THE FIRST FAMILY

OF

OUTSIDERS

Beyond Autism, ADHD, Apples and Angst –

Finding Our Family as We Journeyed

Through the South Carolina State Parks

Spring H. Slagle

ISBN-13:978-0692430668 (Ultimate Outsider)
ISBN-10:0692430660

DEDICATION

Dedicated to the People, Places and Stories of the
South Carolina State Parks.

CONTENTS

Acknowledgments

Thanks to Ranger Phil and the amazing employees of the South Carolina Department of Parks, Recreation and Tourism for issuing the Ultimate Outsider Challenge. Thanks to the wonderful rangers and staff of each of the 47 South Carolina State Parks for welcoming us into your beautiful and wild places. Thanks to Chris for helping with the edits. Thank you to my sweet husband Sam for all the encouragement and love. Thanks especially to our adventuresome children: Ben, Wet Foot, Thoreau and Little Legs for coming with us on this journey. Thank you for taking up the challenge and making it possible for us to become the First Family of Ultimate Outsiders.

1

ULTIMATE OUTSIDERS

I hate watching my children's souls being sucked out through electronic screens and into the unknowable world of the web. Ironic, I know, as I key in this text. And yet, I hope I am not alone in my loathing of the electronic Pied Pipers. We parents stumble through the early mornings, coffee cups sloshing and eyes flitting back to the ever present microwave clock as we rush our young ones through a routine of cereal, basic hygienics, backpacks and bus. We spend the next few hours separated by miles of interstate and mountains of responsibility only to unite again over supper and screens.

I stare at those stupid screens growing out of my children's hands and reflecting off of their beautiful faces. I watch the process of the deepening hypnosis. There isn't a loving parent who hasn't envisioned hurtling an i-device through the window and into the path of an oncoming train.

I WANT MY CHILDREN BACK!!!

But how? How can a mother woo her dear ones back from the world of apples, droids and galaxies?

It is at the moment of deepest desperation that we humans remember what is most dear and basic. We remember what saved us and we pray that it is strong enough to save our prodigy.

I remembered the trails. My happiest and most fulfilled days were spent as a teenager hiking the gentle Appalachian slopes of northeast Tennessee. The creek, the hills, the trees combined to exert monumental power.

Nature has demanded humanity's attention since the beginning of time. It has taken pen prisoner and captivated souls. The basic elements of wood, soil, water and rock would perhaps be the only things powerful enough to steal my children back from the land of microchips and ear buds.

We began with a walk. It was a gentle hike and meant to introduce the children to longer distances and different terrains. Over the next several months, we trekked asphalt, gravel, sand, dirt, puddles and creeks. We explored history, geography, geology, biology, religion, philosophy and psychology. We opened up a different world together as a family.

We set a goal. We would, as a part of the South Carolina Ultimate

Outsider Program, explore every state park in South Carolina. Our state has 47 state parks. Each provides diversity of natural and cultural wealth and beauty. There are swamps, beaches, mountains and lakes that present themselves for discovery and adventure. The parks had just launched a challenge for people to tour each park in the system - all 47. At journey's end, the explorers would be bequeathed the title of "Ultimate Outsider"! The cool title alone would have been worth the trek.

Curious. Accept the Ultimate Outsider Challenge and welcome my children back into the intimacy of family. I had had enough of being cast out of my children's experiences in favor of fickle technology. I laid out the task. We, as a family, were ready to become Ultimate Outsiders.

2

INTRODUCTIONS

The gauntlet had been thrown down! We were doing this! We would explore each park, acquire its individual stamp in our park guide book and thereby become Ultimate Outsiders.

Every parent feels the pressure to save their family from ambivalence. My husband and I feel the pressure even more intently. Our oldest son is a teenager with severe autism accompanied by behavioral, communicative, social and intellectual challenges. Day to day life is hard. None of us can make it through individually. Our only hope of preserving some amount of stability is to work as a team. Our family, the six of us, is a team. We must make it through together.

Introductions are necessary for politeness sake. You must know whose foolhardiness you are bearing witness to.

We christened ourselves the Ramblers. We are an unlikely group of underdogs who should never have accepted this challenge. There are six of us: me, my husband and our four children. Could we pull this off? Absolutely! I think....and if we can so can anybody!

The Children:

Wet Foot

Her name was earned during an unfortunate creek crossing in which she ended up with a soggy squishy tennis shoe. Yes, you read that right. I did say tennis shoe. Due to fashion trends, Wet Foot, who was thirteen when we began our adventure refused hiking boots for the vast majority of our explorations. She maneuvered an iPod truce of sorts whereby she did carry her device but used it to snap pictures of our journeys without connection to cell or Wi-Fi. All she was able to do was document our journey.

Thoreau

His first name was "Tree Hugger" but he found this offensive. We offered "Thoreau" and he was pleased. Thoreau fits my quiet ten year old son. He loves nature, hikes well, and never misses an opportunity to point out a rock, snake or lizard. He documented his journey through his drawings. There is always a great deal running through Thoreau's quiet presence.

Little Legs

She was eight when we began our journeys through the woods and though her legs were short, she was perhaps the toughest hiker of us all. She is skittish of the more unsavory aspects of nature...those being ticks, snakes and poison ivy. Little Legs is mighty in that she has conquered up to eight miles of trail in one day with legs that must take two steps for every one of ours. She is endurance personified.

Big Ben von Gilbert

Now this is where we Ramblers get interesting. Ben was fifteen as we began our adventure. He has severe autism. Despite his many cognitive and behavioral challenges, he has embraced hiking completely and the parks particularly. He is ambulatory and loves to be on the move. Hiking makes so much sense to him. Like many on the autism spectrum, he is a visual thinker and so loves the clearly defined trails blazed and marked with easy to spot colors and arrows. He is uninhibited and expresses his opinions loudly. On the trail, no one cares or is frightened. He can be himself without causing others to be uncomfortable. If anything, his loud laughter keeps the snakes away that his sister Little Legs so detests. Big Ben has a penchant for knowing and announcing the time. He reminded us of the sun's passing throughout our excursions. He helped to keep our party on schedule and to know when to turn back. We have never been stuck on the trail overnight.

Anchor

He is my husband of twenty years, 41, kind, patient and wonderful. We were college sweethearts. He is my best friend and so very much more. Together, we have witnessed and traveled through life's beauty and terror. He is an Anchor to our family and to me. He also runs lead on the trails.

Roz

That would be me. I tried to name myself "Songbird" in honor of the many rounds of "Rise and Shine" that I perform for the children as they get up in the morning. Sometimes though, the right trail name chooses you.

Little Legs and I run sweep (last) during our hikes. I make sure no one gets left behind and am generally in charge of the first aid kit, snacks and deciding which trail to conquer on which day. The children of course tried to pick on one another and generally cause angst and agitation while we hiked. They soon realized that I was right behind them and always watching their escapades. After they learned that they would have to be more creative or give up annoying each other altogether, they gave me the trail name "Roz" from *Monsters, Inc.* According to my dear ones, I was "watching...always watching."

So, introductions made. You'll get to know more about us as you read about our adventures. Boots Up, Friends! Let's Go!

3

BEGINNINGS – ROSE HILL STATE HISTORIC SITE

We began our Ultimate Outsider Quest at Rose Hill State Historic Site. It was perhaps the most unlikely place of all of the 47 possible destinations to begin our journey.

Even history would suggest that Rose Hill is an unlikely place to join into anything. Rose Hill is the home of William Gist better known as South Carolina's "Secession Governor." Wary of the young nation's intrusiveness into individual state affairs, Gist led the political charge in South Carolina towards secession from the Union. He was so adamant regarding his political beliefs that he named his child, "States Rights Gist." That is the actual name William gave his son and had printed in the family Bible which is one of the many treasures preserved and shown to those who visit the historic mansion.

Rose Hill stands upon the very unlikely site of Union, South Carolina. The home looks like it should stand among its historical peers overlooking the Charleston Harbor. Yet, Rose Hill solemnly and silently presides over the outskirts of Union between Columbia and Spartanburg. I can't think that Gist loved that his city and county bore the name "Union."

For us, the Gist mansion was a most unlikely beginning point for our journey. Our trek around the parks was shaped by Ben's tolerance levels and we knew this would push him. This was Ben's first historic home tour. He had, of course, been to museums but a historic home is very different from a museum.

Museums are not quiet places. They are full of movement and noise as visitors freely explore interactive exhibits. You are allowed to pace yourself and move on from those exhibits that are of less interest to you to those that your group finds more appealing. A historic home is fundamentally different. It does not merely house artifacts; it is an artifact. A historic home demands respect and repose. It has rules. One may not run about; one may not wander from room to room; one may not touch.

Touring a historic home is difficult for any child. We were asking Ben who struggles in everyday social situations to do the near impossible.

And yet, don't expect this to be a tale of woe. Rose Hill is after all one of South Carolina's State Parks.

We arrived and the children straightway discovered the large bell in front of the park office. They had great fun ringing it by hanging off of the rope pull. The interpreter at the historic site saw my panic and laughingly assured me that bell ringing was encouraged at Rose Hill.

Before we began our tour, Anchor and I gathered our sweet ones together for a potty run. The bathrooms were located just off the parking lot in a separate structure. Indoor plumbing came about long after Rose Hill rose to prominence. To call the structure an outhouse would be entirely unjust. It was a cabin with a spacious front room leading to its two modern and well maintained toileting facilities.

After finding excellent bathrooms, I dared to be more optimistic regarding the success of our tour as a whole. It's the little things that inspire our journey.

God had smiled on us and Rose Hill was at the moment strangely deserted of guests. My parents had joined us for this visit. My mother loves taking pictures and my father loves asking questions. The interpreter met us on the mansion's front porch and explained the history of the Gist mansion and how the park system had acquired it. The interpreter treated our small group just as if we had been the governor and her entourage and spared no detail of her narration. We all listened and followed from the porch to the foyer while the interpreter explained more of who the Gist family was and how the parks had determined the original color of the paint in the hallway.

Ben was struggling. He was finding little value in the framed Order of Secession that was displayed in the foyer. He began to loudly declare, "Sad." Anchor gave our son the Veggie Tale book which was usually a great distractor. "You're OK. Doing a good job. First house, then lunch."

Yeah. We had attempted a tour of a historic home before lunch. I have had finer moments. It was our mistake but it did not help Ben's mood.

The interpreter continued to lead us through the house. She gave Anchor and Ben sufficient space and grace but did not miss a beat of her narrative. My father kept her busy with a slew of questions regarding the house, its history and its contents. My mother took pictures as I glanced towards Ben and Anchor with worried eyes. I prayed Ben could last through the rest of the tour. His laments were getting louder. He reached out to try to scratch and bite Anchor. Anchor dodged. We have dealt with those behaviors before. Anchor quietly repeated, "No thanks. First tour, then lunch."

Ben shot Anchor a warning look but seemed to calm down a bit. We were OK for a moment and then we entered the dining room. The dining table was decorated with very realistic looking fake fruit. Ben LOVES fruit. He wanted some. Anchor tried to explain that the fruit was not real. "First tour, then lunch."

The ranger proceeded through her interpretation of the property. She did not vary her pace or her persona. If she was uncomfortable with Ben's behaviors, she did not show it.

We followed her upstairs as we continued our tour. It seemed ironic to watch our motley crew ascend such a lovely grand staircase. Still, up we went. We explored the elegant bedroom of Mr. and Mrs. Gist and then proceeded to the children's nursery decorated with period toys. There was a diminutive doll house, a crib with baby clothes and a ball and bat. My own children were entranced – all except for Ben who did not understand that his aggressive behaviors were not having their desired effect of escape. Anchor kept patience and grace. He was quietly repeating, "No thanks. First tour, then lunch."

We were out on the upstairs balcony and then inside again and through the ball room. Little Leg's eyes lit up as she imagined all the grand affairs that had transpired here. My father inquired as to every small detail of the music that would have been played to entertain the guests. Ben's temper was rising as the party stopped so that the ranger could keep up with my father's many many questions. Our tour guide was the most calm of us all and did not appear hurried nor perceivably uncomfortable. Ben was learning that sometimes he must wait but Anchor's hands were paying the price in scratches. The tour continued back downstairs and the ranger completed her rendition of the Gist family history.

Angels sang as we stepped out into the sunlight. Ben had made it! So had Anchor! As promised, "First tour, then lunch." We were off.

Lunch was a wonderful discovery. We drove from Rose Hill and came upon the Bantam Chef. The older looking building without a nationally known name and mascot might have caused unease for some but we noticed the overflowing parking lot. That parking lot attested to the quality of the Bantam Chef. Locals knew where the good food was. We threw our trust to the community wisdom and pulled in.

We were greeted warmly with a southern, "Hey, what can I get for ya?" We beheld a smiling welcome from the lady at the cash register. "We have everything but spaghetti," she laughed. Ben requested, "Cheeseburger" which seemed like a good idea to all of us. We filled up on cheeseburgers, fries and ice cream. There are some meals that are worth time spent sweating in the gym. Trust me, this was one of those.

4

MUSGROVE MILL –
HISTORY MADE FUN!

Musgrove Mill is surprisingly close to Columbia. A few short miles on Interstate 26 led us to Clinton, South Carolina and Musgrove Mill.

Musgrove Mill cured me of any fear I may have had of introducing Ben to historic sites. Our state parks are comprised of three essential elements: story, place and people. Musgrove Mill brought all three elements together beautifully in a way that was fun and exciting for my boisterous brood!

We saw the stamp at the kiosk in front of the building. Musgrove Mill immediately got extra creativity points as they had placed their stamp inside a historic looking saddlebag attached to the wooden sign. Having obtained the necessary stamp, we proceeded into the main building. As we crossed the welcoming front porch, I made a mental note of its several inviting rocking chairs that seemed to beckon weary visitors. We were greeted immediately by a great open room housing a large lighted table with buttons. Ben loves buttons. He headed straight for it.

My own attention was given to Ranger Dawn who straightway called out a hearty Southern "Hello! Welcome to Musgrove Mill!" as we crossed into the foyer. We all fell in love with Ranger Dawn. Here was a lady who did not patronize but recognized the value and intelligence of youth.

She gave special attention to each of my four children simultaneously. I can't explain how she did it and I know it doesn't make much sense. My only explanation is that she is just that good.

Ben approached Ranger Dawn and promptly broke through the proper social space that people commonly observe. My tall lanky boy was nose to nose with Ranger Dawn. He grabbed her hands and held them. "Come Out and Play," he greeted. He was repeating the slogan for the South Carolina State Park system. Instinctively, I reached for Ben to pull him back an inch or two but Ranger Dawn just smiled at my son. "He's not bothering me," she reassured. She turned all of her attention to Ben, "How are you?"

"I'm fine," he replied.

Ranger Dawn accepted us. She did more than that. She genuinely welcomed us as a typical family of visitors. Ranger Dawn, as a representative of the South Carolina Parks and of Musgrove Mill State Historic Site, welcomed us and then introduced us to the history and significance of South Carolina's newest park.

Musgrove Mill had been home to Edward Musgrove and his family long ago during the days leading up to the American Revolutionary War. The exhibits tell the story of Mr. Musgrove, his family, his property and its involvement in the American Revolution. The battle at Musgrove Mill was one in which the Patriots were badly outnumbered by the Tories but managed a "win" via superior strategy.

Ranger Dawn explained the exhibits relating to life in the backcountry of South Carolina during the days of the Revolution. She showed us a map of the battle and told us of the interpretive trails which we could explore. She spent an incredible amount of time with us. She noticed Thoreau's interest in the musket that was twice as big as he was.

Ranger Dawn taught Thoreau how to hold and spark the musket. My young backcountry Patriot has never forgotten that moment. Ranger Dawn allowed herself to be a conduit between child and history via a musket.

Since that first visit, Ranger Dawn has helped to make Musgrove Mill one of the best South Carolina State Parks for children. She has sewn period clothing for children of various ages and sizes so that they can try them on and further experience history on a personal level. Musgrove Mill has a unique understanding that children must be interested in history so that the story itself can survive. With this in mind, the rangers have gone to great pains to make history fun for the children that visit. Musgrove Mill added an exhibit of hands on period children's games. Children are expected to play in the great open room at Musgrove Mill. The room reverberates with laughter as kids and parents play nine pins, shuttlecock or the game of graces.

The secret of Musgrove Mill is how much learning happens as the children play.

5

THROUGH THE LANDSFORD LOOKING GLASS

Landsford Canal is perhaps the most beautiful of all of the 47 South Carolina State Parks.

Idyllic.

I kept looking around and wondering if I had indeed stepped through the looking glass and been transported into Wonderland.

Most of the visitors we saw at Landsford were families enjoying each other's company over a picnic lunch. A few were preparing their kayaks to survey the slow moving river. We passed all these fellow day trippers and chose to explore the Canal Trail.

We had just begun our walk when we saw a beautiful girl in a flowing dress standing amid the greenery and flowers of the trail. She smiled and ushered us on. Real life emulated fairy tale. We did a double take. The princess was certainly there before us. She was posing in her prom finery flanked by her proud mother and her rather fussy photographer.

I felt we were underdressed in our hiking regalia. Still, on we tramped quietly and humbly past the young beauty and her entourage. There had to have been a magical portal that we had stumbled through. This was a whole world of splendor.

The girl was enchanting but even she could not compare to the ornate simplicity of spring's canvas displayed for us along the Canal Trail. The early afternoon sunlight illuminated the foliage around us and breathed ethereal radiance onto the trail itself. Butterflies flitted all around us. I'm very serious. Butterflies literally danced and flew before, beside and behind us guiding our way down the trail. They quietly commanded us to stop and marvel at the overall wonder of this place that enveloped us.

As we regained our footing and once again journeyed on, we came across an intricate repository of stonework. The Irish stonemasons from the early

nineteenth century had left their mark in the form of locks and walls and bridges. Their work had once conducted the river along this trail before the waters shifted and left the trail to us. Evidence of the stone masons' labors still stood. The stones were beautifully eerie and seemed to have grown naturally among the grass and trees of the wood. We could almost hear the shouts of the masons and the groans of the laborers as we walked between the high walls where water had once passed.

Landsford is a poetic, romantic place.

Alas, I am a mom with four children who were all learning how to hike together. Reality can sometimes snuff the romantic glow.

Wet Foot was not in the best of moods. Her teenage angst clouded the glories of nature in favor of the trials of adolescence.

Thoreau was quiet and observant. In a most everyday voice he said, "There's a snake." And so there was. A shiver ran down my spine but luckily this serpent was small and slithered on its way through the undergrowth beside us.

Ben kept track of the time and was happy to be pressing forward along the trail.

Little Legs grabbed me tight as she heard Thoreau's casual identification of the snake.

We kept walking guided by the trail which was by then deserted save for our ragtag group. Nature did not seem to mind. She welcomed us and winked as we kept exploring this picturesque juxtaposition of natural wonder and human craftsmanship.

Landsford Canal is the secret hideaway of the elusive Rocky Shoals Water Lily - a rare flower which graces this river for only a few weeks in early May. I'm sure the lily in bloom is breath taking. The flower pridefully displays herself in the river beckoning visitors crowd a viewing stand and admire her finery. Meanwhile, the rest of Landsford smiles and sighs and is grateful to give the Landsford Lily her due. Landsford's trail, her native animals, minerals, mosses and trees lie back in the luxury of anonymity. To the odd visitor who explores Landsford more deeply, the park shyly opens and allows herself to be known and appreciated.

We surprised Landsford with our off season visit before the lilies bloomed. We pushed past her trail head and urged her to become known to us. We were richly rewarded. Landsford kissed our spirits and changed us. She surprised us with her loveliness and grace. She took our admiration and respect for the South Carolina State Parks to a new place. It was here at Landsford that we began to fall in love.

6

ANDREW JACKSON STATE PARK - THE WEDDING CAKE AND THE MUSEUM

We managed to stumble out of the portal and were now transported from the Wonderland of Landsford Canal into the stark reality of the parking lot. We had no choice but to travel on.

It was almost 5:00 when we pulled into the parking area of Andrew Jackson State Park. Again, we were underdressed. A wedding party had assembled at the large shelter just beside where we had parked our minivan. What a beautiful idea. The park was gorgeous now in the first throes of spring. The reception was already set up picnic style outside the shelter and the shelter itself was adorned with white garland. The park's trees and flowers complimented the wedding party's own bouquets.

We quietly (or as quietly as a family of six could) spilled from our van and made for the park office to obtain our stamp. Anchor and Little Legs stamped our Outsider page while I attempted to keep Ben from crashing the wedding - more to the point - the wedding cake.

Proximity was our difficulty as Ben kept dragging me closer to the delicate, decadent and no doubt delicious cake. A quick scan for diversions revealed historic buildings and a museum. I suddenly felt that this was a great time to explore the history of Andrew Jackson State Park while I prayed that the wedding guests would quickly consume every morsel of that scrumptious looking cake.

Thankfully, the museum had not yet locked up for the evening. The rangers and interpreters take their task of sharing their park's story very seriously and even the latest visitors were warmly welcomed.

I continue to be amazed at the overall quality of the exhibits at the state park museums. Andrew Jackson State Park celebrates the early life of the former frontiersman, soldier, politician and president. The exhibit opens by depicting what Andrew Jackson's early home may have looked like in the backcountry of the new frontier. We saw the corner with the washing implements and the simple but charming blanket chest. We went on to the combination kitchen / dining / bed / living room. Little Legs was particularly intrigued by the rope bed. The ranger saw the young girl's interest and fueled it. "Go ahead," the ranger instructed. "You can sit on it." Little Legs was amazed. Her eyes widened as she carefully sat upon the side of the bed. That was the moment

frontier life came alive to Little Legs. Through the exhibit and especially through the kind and watchful eyes of the ranger at Andrew Jackson,

Little Legs came to understand the meanness of frontier life and the truth behind the adage, "Sleep Tight; Don't Let the Bed Bugs Bite."

Authentic, hands on exhibits like those at Andrew Jackson convey the meaning of historic living conditions to these little ones. Little Legs routinely slept in a plush bed in the company of a menagerie of stuffed bears, kittens and bunnies. This clean but sparse room was so different from anything she had come across before. It had to be shown and experienced to be believed by my daughter or any modern day child. I loved seeing the moment of understanding as she sat on the rope bedside and scanned that plain room.

Ben, however, was not happy. His mind had not let go of the image of wedding cake and he was not inclined to tarry here at the museum when cake was so very near. To make matters worse, there was fake food on the replica of Jackson's table. But Ben didn't even try to eat this fake food. While the meal displayed would have made an excellent repast, it served as no real comparison to wedding cake. We had to leave the museum to visit again another day. We would come back to more fully explore the videos, the uniforms and the artifacts regarding Jackson's later years. That was an option and a miracle. The museum was free and would wait for us to come back.

A fantastic aspect of the parks is the freedom it allowed us. Ben's behavioral difficulties usually required us to avoid places where we felt he might have a meltdown. If he became upset, we would have to take him out and thus forfeit our admission fee. The parks offer exceptional people the opportunity to view exceptional exhibits on their own terms. If Ben was having a difficult time, we did as much as he could stand and then regrouped to plan another visit for another day.

The ranger smiled a reassuring smile at Ben and told us we were welcome anytime.

We left the museum and spied the wedding. The reception was going strong with cake and karaoke. Ben was watchful. We knew it would be difficult to get him to the van in order to leave without him breaking away to sample the cake. Luckily, Andrew Jackson has a set of trails to explore. There was no better time. A walk in the woods and another beside the pond passed the time. Our adventure at Andrew Jackson ended with no wedding cake calamities. Anchor and I celebrated victory. We gathered the children back into the van and headed off to Lake Wateree.

7

LAKE WATEREE - IN PURSUIT OF A GRANOLA BAR

First Landsford Canal, then Andrew Jackson and now we traveled on to Lake Wateree. Geographically, our order was ill planned. Lake Wateree was the closest to us and Andrew Jackson furthest away. But Landsford closed first, then Andrew Jackson and finally Lake Wateree, so our path had been determined.

It had been a good day overall exploring the history of the Irish canal workers and that of the backcountry frontiersmen of colonial South Carolina. It was somehow odd to leave the echoes of history and travel to a park that emphasized fishing and camping. I tried to excite the children to the final leg of our day's park adventure. I told them about a flyer I had found online as I had researched Lake Wateree. The rangers at Wateree wanted to encourage more physical activity and exploration from their guests and had issued a challenge. The guests should hike out to the far reaches of the park's nature trail and take a picture. The guests would then bring that picture to the tackle shop/gift store/office and receive a granola bar.

That incentive was enough. Wet Foot's eyes lit up. She had been given a challenge and hope of a prize.

Please know that our children have had many granola bars and other snacks throughout their lifetimes. Wet Foot was fond of granola but not generally overwhelmed by its goodness. I do not claim to understand everything there is to know about a young teenage girl. I do know that something changed when she heard about the promise of a "nature snack". The girl lit up and transformed into a woman on a mission. Wet Foot turned tyrant and attempted to drive her siblings on down the trail faster and faster. The poor things had already hiked the trails at Landsford Canal and Andrew Jackson. Wet Foot did not care. She kept at it. "Come on," she commanded.

I watched her attempt to motivate her charges as the sun was setting. I thought it best to let her know, "Sweetie, we may not make it back before the shop closes."

"Oh yes we will," was her spirited response as the sun sank into a glamorous finale across the lake. The sky was alight with bright orange and red clouds which calmed into sedate shades of blue and purple. I could see stars beginning to appear.

Little Legs was panting.

I was not quite confident in the success of Wet Foot's quest.

Still, my teenage daughter kept her eyes glued to the clock on her iPod. It showed we had ten minutes until the rangers would desert the store. "We can make it," Wet Foot whispered intently.

We didn't make it. We were about ten minutes late.

Wet Foot approached the darkened window in disbelief and sat down on a bench just beside the locked entryway. Her face bled disappointment. I saw my child sitting on the hard utilitarian bench unconsciously shaking her head in sadness as she realized the clock's victory.

I couldn't help it. I giggled. I had to. I laughed out loud. My daughter glared. Still I laughed and now pointed to the sign just above her head in the tackle shop window. "Happy Camper," it read. Yes, we got a picture.

8

UNEXPECTED TREASURE - LAKE GREENWOOD STATE PARK

I was less than enthusiastic about our visit to Lake Greenwood State Park.

"I guess maybe we could do it as a picnic," I told my husband. I had pored over maps of the parks and roads in hopes of finding a way to combine Lake Greenwood with another park. There wasn't a good way. We had already visited the more local parks and that left Lake Greenwood all by itself on the map.

I sighed. Lake Greenwood was more of a recreational area - a place to enjoy the day on your boat. That is wonderful but we don't have a boat. The day itself did not soothe me. It was uncharacteristically cool for April and was very windy too. To be honest, I wasn't even sure we could pull off a picnic.

Unapologetically unassuming, Lake Greenwood lay about an hour past our church and in the opposite direction of all I knew. We scouted around for a picnic table and found one near the playground. We got the kids together and trekked to the lakeside spot and tried to enjoy ourselves though we were being battered by the wind. We chased cups and napkins and children. The kids complained about the significant chill that pervaded our picnic area. Ben began to pick up on my discontent. He was less than understanding about the delay of his food as we fought the wind to prepare his sandwich. Ben began to exhibit aggressive behavior. He was frustrated and wondered if biting and scratching would help to improve the situation as a whole. It didn't. My eyes began to well up and I looked over to Anchor. His look agreed with mine. We put everything including the children back into the van as we declared, "Car Picnic!" We did make sure to proudly display our park passport entry tag in our front window and took pictures. We were trying our best to salvage the experience as we munched sandwiches in the Kia.

We finished our repast and now needed to get the Lake Greenwood stamp. We scoured the shore for kiosks. No luck. My frustration level continued to build. We decided to go find the ranger station. We drove over to the unassuming building with the flag in front and a small garden beside it. We parked, entered the office, and then....

I SAW IT! Cue Angel Songs!

I am a nerd - self professed. I have a bachelor's and a master's degree in history. The South Carolina parks are about place, story and people. Of those, the stories (which are about the people and the place) interest me the most. We opened the front door of the ranger station and entered one of the most amazing stories that the park service has to offer.

Before us lay a museum dedicated to the Civilian Conservation Corps.

34

In true showman style, the exhibit opened humbly without a hint of the greatness it had in store. We ducked behind a partition into a darkened cubicle where a screen displayed newsreel that set up the crisis of the Great Depression and the hope that FDR brought with the formation of the CCC.

On through the exhibit, we were hurled through time as we sat by the ancient radio which looked new in a meager but clean kitchen circa the 1930s and listened to FDR's Fireside Chat. We walked on and saw more newsreels depicting the young men proudly serving their nation as servants of the CCC. South Carolina camps were showcased,

particularly those that have now become South Carolina State Parks. Among those featured were Myrtle Beach, Edisto and Poinsett.

All of this was only to set the stage. The exhibit emptied into a makeshift classroom as the Corps sought to educate its conscripts on the value of soil conservation and the environmentally sound and conscientious methods of building. Stools were set up and held mighty volumes detailing parkitecture which was at the time a new practice of using ready natural resources to build park structures. This parkitecture with its signature wood and stonework mark every South Carolina CCC acquired park.

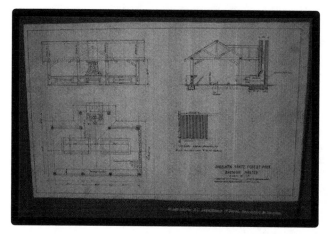

We were ushered through the elements of environment, culture and conservation all featuring the South Carolina State Parks like Lee, Poinsett, Aiken and Barnwell. We were shown the forest green uniform and the hard heavy tools of the tree army. We were then introduced to the veterans of the CCC via interviews and newsreel. I watched my little ones listening to elderly men recounting their glory days in the park army. My children are young and did not pick up on everything. Even so, they noted the pride that shone in the eyes of the aged men. These men knew that even as their hair was thinning and their feet were slowing that they had made a real difference. The men of the Civilian Conservation Corps had given valuable service to their country. More interview stations sought our attention and more artifacts drew us on. We learned of pranks pulled. The boys of the CCC surprised their fellow tree soldiers by lugging their mattresses up onto the rafters of the cabins. We heard about the fun that was had as the camps broke out into baseball games. We saw old men's eyes sparkle as they sat beside their wives and told how they had first met at the community dances put on for the corps. We learned how lives were bettered as $20 from every $25 monthly (yes, monthly) CCC check went back home to help hold property and family together as the Depression ravaged on.

We left the exhibit marveling that such a place existed and that it was hiding here at Lake Greenwood. Yes, Lake Greenwood was a CCC camp but so were many others. I further marveled that there had been no signage of the exhibit that had all the character and quality of a large museum.

Months later, I learned the secret of Lake Greenwood. It was so important that I again made the pilgrimage to the park to pay tribute to the place that was the most fitting setting for the CCC memories to be kept.

As you drive into Lake Greenwood State Park, the road is flanked by tremendous pines that reach heavenward. They shed their needles to provide a cradle to the most appropriate memorial of the Civilian Conservation Corps. The spirits and ghosts of the CCC are active here in this pine forest where the men of this camp last left their work. Great stones litter the ground in the forest just off the side of the road that leads into the park. They were left there at the end of the day on December 6, 1942. The men had toiled all day. They had chiseled, moved and crafted the beginnings of a wall to greet guests coming to the park. This was to be their finishing touch and final mark of their work here at Lake Greenwood. December 7, 1942 brought news of Japan's attack on Pearl Harbor. The men of Lake Greenwood Civilian Conservation Corps ran to the defense of their country and so abandoned these mighty stones to lie as a testament to what the CCC had been and what it had achieved.

Many credit FDR and his administration for ushering America out of the Great Depression. I think he knew that is was these men and their families that took the heavy load and fashioned something great out of the boulders that were weighing our country down. The men of the CCC came together over sweat and labored for American's resurgence and then for her defense. The CCC, supported by their communities and their families, left the living monuments that are now some of the finest state parks in the country. What a precious gift to all that America is. They preserved the essential elements of America by creating places where citizens and wildlife could come together in beauty, respect and admiration. The work of the Civilian Conservation Corps is a testament to the best piece of who we are as a country.

The stones that lay at Lake Greenwood State Park, the memories and stories stored and shared here...these are fitting tribute. This is the fitting place.

9

CHESTER STATE PARK – CALLS OF NATURE

It had threatened rain all day. We hadn't counted on being able to go out to a park at all that Saturday. By afternoon, the weather wasn't too bad, our chores were done and the children's moods were good. More than that, the children were becoming used to spending their Saturdays in the parks. They were expecting it. It was becoming a wonderful routine.

The same boredom that used to bring nagging about playing electronics was now beckoning us into the wilds of the parks. I did a quick check and realized that Chester State Park wasn't far and that we had yet to explore it.

The fog hung in the trees as we entered the park. It promised cool refreshment from an otherwise hot and humid southern spring day. We stopped for the stamp and the rangers made sure to show us their pride - the original Chester State Park sign from the 1930s. It had been left over from the park's birth at the hands of the CCC, the Civilian Conservation Corps, who labored to see this place as a retreat for nearby residents.

We left the rangers and the sign and went on to explore the nature trail. It was odd to see the park largely deserted. The weather reports alone must have scared the majority of visitors off. The day itself maintained a gentle blanketing feel.

We found the nature trail and followed it by the lake. We took a moment to peek inside the boat house, the iconic yet approachable resting place for the park's jon boats. The children's eyes lit up with excitement. Wet Foot got the first word in, "I really want to do this, Mom!" It was wonderful to see her express the same amount of enthusiasm over a jon boat as she would have earlier expressed over her iPod. A couple of boats were already on the water. They had been taken out by locals who would have their families believe they were fishing. Actually, they were joking, laughing and calling back and forth to one another and giving the grateful fish plenty of advance warning of the whereabouts of their boats and lines. We decided to let the fisherman enjoy their outing but promised that we would soon get a jon boat for the children to take out.

We were fairly quiet - quiet for us anyway. We explored the small hill in the clearing capped by a large CCC shelter. As always, we stopped and stared. The stonework was unreal. It shone of the pride of the young men who had fashioned it.

We went on past a set of quite slippery granite steps designed to assist hikers as they trudged down a small incline. Today though, the granite was wet. Wet Foot's tennis shoes caught the rock's slick surface. She plopped down hard. I was behind my daughter and saw just how hard she hit. My Mama instinct activated. I was afraid she might have broken something. As I approached, her terrified face fueled my alarm. My child tremulously reached behind and felt her back pocket. The slightest touch of relief passed over her eyes. "It didn't break," she whispered as she protectively inspected her iPod.

She stood and declared herself fine though she did walk with a slower and more measured pace for the rest of the afternoon. She meandered back to where Little Legs and I hiked behind the rest of the family. My darling daughter maintained that she just wanted the pleasure of our company but I could tell she was still stiff.

Chester seemed apologetic now for causing injury. The trail ahead was decorated with delicate white dogwood petals. The trees, the petals, and the mist came together to create an atmosphere both surreal and romantic. On up by the pond's edge, we saw a Canadian goose and still further on we spied an elegant egret. The owls called to each other adding to the atmosphere of the late afternoon. Everything was slow and still and lovely.

"Uh, guys," Thoreau interrupted the holy serenity. "I really have to go to the bathroom." One look at our son who was awkwardly shifting his weight back and forth made us believe him.

"Sweetie, the bathroom is a mile back. Can you hold it?"

"Uhhhhh.....I'll try," came the panicked yet comic response.

Thoreau is an old soul but is still at the age which requires every bathroom reference to be punctuated by giggles.

"Oh, I shouldn't laugh," he giggled painfully as we turned around.

Thoreau's dear sisters noted their poor brother's distress. I would like to say that they were understanding, sweet and kind to their brother in his plight. That would be a lie and I will not insult your intelligence with such an unbelievable falsehood. They poured out comments about water, rain and waterfalls. It did not help that the poor boy was surrounded by trees dripping rainwater from their heavily laden leaves. Thoreau giggled and groaned and strained to retain control of the situation.

Our journey back was much faster than our initial trek had been. Even in our haste, we remembered Wet Foot's earlier dilemma and were mindful and respectful of the slippery granite steps. Wet Foot kept fingering her lucky iPod and walked with a bit of a limp.

Triumph!

No one was happier to get back to the shelter and the bath house than my sweet son.

As I waited on him to relieve himself, I thought about how he might recount his weekend adventures to his buddies at school.

Friends: "What did you do this weekend?"

Thoreau: "Went on a hike with my family."

Friends: "It was raining."

Thoreau: "I know. It was cool until I had to use the bathroom." (I prefer to imagine that all proper terms would be used in a ten year old boys' conversation about toileting. I know better but I prefer to imagine it that way.)

Friends: "Oh, man. That sounds horrible." (See above note about how I prefer to imagine boys' conversations.)

Thoreau: "Nah, it was really fun."

Or Wet Foot's...

Friends: "Are you ok?"

Wet Foot: "Yeah, I just fell."

Friends: "Where? When?"

Wet Foot: "It's all good. Over the weekend on these big rock steps at Chester State Park."

Friends: "Where's that?"

Wet Foot: "It's one of the parks my family is hiking through. It's ok though. My iPod didn't break."

And her friends would understand the importance of that.

We were making memories. Bonding. These moments are so few. Potty jokes, rain hikes, falls and spills, love, laughter….

Watching the kids run and play and then sitting still trying to coax a fish onto their line, wow. I watched my children in the cool fog. I saw my family walking along the lake shore and I smiled. We were doing it. We were achieving so much more than the title of Ultimate Outsider. We were falling in love with one another, getting to know and like each other individually and enjoying who we were together. We had "Come Out to Play" …and we were having so much fun!

10

SESQUI AND THE CITY

Wet Foot still has a difficult time saying "Sesquicentennial" ....so now she just hams it up and overemphasizes her mispronunciations. Sesqui was a park we had explored over and over again throughout the years we have been in South Carolina. It is relatively close to our home and was always an easy park to escape to.

Sesqui is the parkiest park of them all. Sesquicentennial is the definitive  state park. Sesqui is a combination of cookouts with charcoaled hamburgers and hot dogs, spirited children chasing and racing on, up and through playgrounds and crowded waters filled with pedal boats and canoes. The park welcomes families, hikers, bikers and campers. Sesqui was built as a recreational outlet for the Columbia area by the Civilian Conservation Corps. A memorial, a boathouse and picnic shelters still mark the CCC's presence there.

Sesqui reminds one of a favorite aunt, the kind with lots of great stuff and a permissive spirit. She is not glamorous but she is constant. Sesqui openly offers adventure, exploration and fun.

We have hiked her sandy trails often. It is a great place to explore even after the rain makes other trails muddy and impassable. The sand drinks the puddles as they form. We have attended programs here and broadened our knowledge about various critters and plants. Once during a program about snakes, one of the reptiles tried to strike Anchor through a glass aquarium. Even though we knew we were safe, the power and force that the reptile threw  at the glass made us jump in fright. We have picnicked and cooked out at Sesqui. We have enjoyed family and have together strolled around the lake. If Sesqui could speak, we would sit with her and reminisce about birthday celebrations and butterfly hunts, about first nights spent under the stars and treasures found in hidden caches. She would captivate with stories. Sesquicentennial is historic. She does possess natural beauty but even more she establishes herself as a definitive and integral part of the Columbia community. She is a portal transferring her visitors from the hurly burly of stress laden traffic commutes into a land of respite. She is an antidote to city life - a place where one can regain perspective, breathe deeply and enjoy the sweet simple luxuries of family and conversation. Sesqui is vital to the Columbia metropolis. Sesqui centers the capital. Sesquicentennial saves the city from itself.

11

THE STILLNESS OF GOODALE

Columbia is at the center and is flanked by three state parks whose central purpose is recreation. Goodale is a secret place unless you happen to live within fifteen miles of Camden. It is so close to the capital and yet is a world apart. You know you are about to enter the secret place when you pass the bison farm on the way to the park.

The morning we visited was rainy and cool. The dogwoods were just coming into bloom. The trail was at first deserted except for us. The rain had been gentle and did not leave much mud - just stillness. We hiked the  trail and our attention fell to the lush low lying ferns just off the trail in the woods. The fronds were decorated with glistening droplets of rain. The wispy fog that had been left by the rain and the delicate white petals of the dogwoods bade us to keep quiet. The children were even subdued. Eventually some bikers passed our silent procession. Hikers generally shirk at the mention of these wheeled trail companions but the mood of the park had pervaded the bikers too. They were swift but silent. They expertly maneuvered around our troop. They smiled and waved knowing that we were sharing the quiet stillness of this place together.

I think the gentle trail must extract the stillness of those she bears. We saw benches along the trail directing us humans to sit and contemplate Goodale's wonders. She had compelled us to quietness. Still, not even Goodale and her well placed benches could command our children to sit in quiet reflection. Absolute stillness is against their nature. We went on.

We emerged from the trail into the low brightness of the morning. We were out into the clearing facing the water that was showing off her adornment of lilies. The children threw off the stillness of the wood and began to come back to themselves. They filled the clearing with laughter and shouts. They raced from the water to the park kiosk. They played and ran around the wooden sign that stands over the old  stone waterwheel. Their youthful spirits rebelled against the stillness.

It had been good to watch these young ones still and quiet in the woods as they had been drawn into the fairy land of sparkling ferns and delicate dogwoods. Now it was a relief to see them being playful. It was a pleasure to hear them laugh and to behold them in the fullness of their youth as they spewed life and energy. It was as if I was watching them wake up. In stillness or play, it was good to see them drawing close to nature's offerings in lieu of the white glow of the unfeeling screen.

In the stillness of Goodale, I had caught a glimpse of something fantastic.

I had been privy to a wonderful moment in the lives of my children. I had watched their spirits grow.

12

THE CATERPILLAR TREE AT WOODS BAY

I remember watching a Ken Burns documentary about the National Parks on our local PBS station. It seemed odd that the fiercest advocate for the Everglades, Marjory Stoneman Douglas, had written, "To be a friend of the Everglades is not necessarily to spend time wandering around out there." She was a petite middle class socialite who was much more accustomed to tea parties than to reptiles and humidity. The documentary spoke her voice via her writings. Her words are quite different than what one might expect from an ardent advocate of the wild place she loved, "I know it's out there and I know its importance. I suppose you could say the Everglades and I have the kind of friendship that doesn't depend on constant physical contact."

And so it is with Woods Bay State Natural Area. By any account, Woods Bay is South Carolina's answer to the deep Florida swamps. Woods Bay beckons the traveler far from the beaten path into Olanta, South Carolina. We didn't know where that was either nor can I now recount for you exactly how to get there. My only advice in finding Woods Bay is to be nice to your GPS and hope it steers you true.

We turned from the main road and passed the ever present state park placard. This same style of sign is present at Rose Hill and Landsford Canal State Parks. Woods Bay has its own personality and is entirely different from either Rose Hill or Landsford Canal. Woods Bay is deep and dark and mysterious.

We were alone on the road. It was dark; the sun was being blocked by the canopy of the trees. Like a perfect movie set, clouds moved in and the sun shrank completely away. It darkened further and cooled. Nature held her breath wondering at our entry into the swamp.

All children are instinctual and Ben is especially so. He breathed in the dark mist and breathed out a foul mood. We pulled up to the parking lot and he began to yell. I came to him to try to help him out of the van and he tried to bite me. Anchor and I exchanged glances wondering how long we would dare tarry here. We were much more wary of our son's behaviors than of seeing gators (though I was very wary of gators too.).

We scouted the kiosk and did not find the stamp. Anchor went to the visitor center to find it closed. Ben, meanwhile, had escalated in his unhappiness. I found a picnic shelter and directed Ben to sit at one end of it while I stayed closer to the other side. The rain came. Anchor and the kiddos except for Ben had all but given up on the stamp when they happened upon another human. She had a key to the visitor center and so we got the stamp. Success! The family was reunited at the picnic shelter. Their smiles left when they rightly perceived the enormity of Ben's ill mood. "Give him some space," I instructed.

We couldn't get back in the van with Ben in this present mood - not when he was like this. We had to wait for him to deescalate. Anchor and I again spoke with our eyes. We scanned the area and together saw the simple sign that pointed the way further on into the swamp. "Boardwalk," it read. The air was still dark but the rain had stopped. The only other person we had seen in the park, the lady who opened the visitor center and stamped our book, had abandoned the place. We shrugged, gathered our children and proceeded towards the boardwalk.

Anchor led with Ben. Thoreau and Wet Foot took center but gravitated toward the rear along with Little Legs and me who were taking our usual place as sweep. Ben was still in a foul mood and alternated yells, hitting his head and trying to lash out against Anchor. My mama instincts were on high alert as we escorted our children through the still black waters of the swamp. We ventured out onto the boardwalk and beheld the Cyprus forest which was beautifully foreboding that day. I expected to hear ominous music begin to play softly to serenade our unlikely parade of explorers.

This would be the perfect time to insert an alligator into the script of our day. There were signs warning of the reptiles. I instructed my little hikers to "Stomp!" So they did. Thoreau and Little Legs stomped hard on the boards and created loud vibrations through the dark water. If any cold blooded critter were to think of attacking my band of children, it would have to fight against a millennium of instinct just to approach us.

"Mom! Stop!" complained my teenage Wet Foot. She wanted to see an alligator. My eyes grew wide with mama fear and my terse reply came out, "You're crazy!" I looked at my sweet Thoreau and Little Legs and directed them to, "Keep Stomping!" They obeyed and helped to keep the native reptiles at bay.

But even in the midst of my fears and of the real and imagined dangers of the swamp, there was wonder and beauty. The still Cyprus laden swamp waters gave way to thick impassable shrubs. They would have been impassible. They were open to us as we continued upon the ever present ribbon of safety embodied by the wooden boardwalk. On we walked past signs describing the strange Carolina Bays, a natural geographic anomaly as yet unexplained by science. Perhaps this place was once witness to a meteor shower. Maybe the great divots in the earth had been caused by aliens. Wonderful, I thought. I imagined a headline, "Family of Six Aspiring Ultimate Outsiders Eaten by Alien Alligators. " Lovely. On we walked past the thick walls of the swamp shrubs, past massive spiders and the occasional lizard, past a lizard caught in a spider's web, past the spider eating the lizard in the web. Is that even possible, I wondered? I have never before nor since seen a spider eating a lizard. On and on we went until the boardwalk abruptly stopped. It could no longer wrestle the swamp and so it simply stopped. This was our boundary.

We turned to retrace our steps and noticed a tree covered — teeming - overcome by caterpillars. Short, fuzzy, black lines moving, undulating, progressing up and up as if to envelop the tall thin spire. Six feet even above the boardwalk, the tree had become possessed and was succumbing to the power of the caterpillar colony. An organized mob of

unexpected dark dashes had gathered on this unassuming tree and now demanded our attention. We stopped and watched and gave the spectacle its due.

Our explorations had taken us to an alien place. Nowhere more than here, in the surreal swamp of Woods Bay, have I felt myself so small and incredibly out of place.

It was a privilege to peep into the world of Woods Bay.

We returned to the van. Ben had over time calmed. We had been to Woods Bay and we were changed. I do not need to go often to visit Woods Bay. It is enough for me to appreciate the wild swamp from my own place. I am content to know that such a place exists and that it is protected.

13

RESTORATION AT LEE STATE PARK

We had all been affected by Woods Bay. How could we have escaped the wildness of that place unscathed? We were uneasy. Woods Bay had reached inside our spirits and touched them with its foreboding presence. I wanted to be done. I wanted to gather my babies and go home.

But I couldn't. The only logical way to accomplish the Ultimate Outsider challenge is to follow the lines of parks and visit all that are within the same area on the same day. Our group was called to press on and so we journeyed to Lee.

We needed Lee that day after Woods Bay. We just didn't know it. The research I had done suggested that Lee was a favorite for equine enthusiasts. We were prepared to make Lee a short stop. Get the stamp, stretch our legs, go home. But Lee had other plans. Lee unexpectedly caught us up in a much needed embrace. Lee refreshed us. Lee comforted us. Lee drew us in and has not yet let us go.

Each park has a spirit about it, something difficult to explain but much more powerful that curb appeal. Each park has a pervasive culture. As you enter the property, you sense it. As you explore further, the air fills with the heart of the place. The park personifies. It swells of gregarious quiet. It smiles; it beckons; it leads.

Lee is a deep park. The road draws you on and on into its center. It is a gift lovingly built by the CCC so that families could come and enjoy the place and refresh their souls. The spirits of those young men who labored here are alive at Lee. You can feel their pride as their ghosts watch children run between the parkitectured shelters and splash in the artesian wells.

We pulled into the parking lot and Anchor went into the office to inquire about the trails. He came back to the van after just a few minutes. He was smiling and shaking his head. He opened the door. "Come on. Everybody out," he instructed. "What?" I asked. Anchor again shook his head and laughed. "The folks here were so excited that we're visiting that they told me to hurry up and get everybody so they can say hi and show the kids the nature center."

Seriously? It was Saturday evening and close to 5:00. It was time for the office to close and yet these rangers were insisting on staying open late to welcome our unexpected visit. We were strangers here and we were nasty and smelly from the rain. There were six of us for goodness sake. Seriously? Yes.

That is what Lee does. The artesian wells were well placed here. They must be a sort of mascot of refreshment and rejuvenation. The waters of the wells and the sweetness of the air have thoroughly infected those who work here with the same sense of welcome and refreshment. The spirit of love and comfort springs from those who love Lee as the water itself springs from those dated wells.

We gathered our children and came to where we were welcomed by two older gentlemen. These men seemed to be straight from Mayberry and wore the biggest "Glad to know you" smiles imaginable. They overwhelmed us with sincere joy as we entered the ranger station/nature center/gift shop. They were thrilled to have the opportunity to welcome us into this park that they loved so much.

Ranger Lester proudly showed us the giant display featuring the native animals and plant species of the watershed. His assistant Rick had carefully prepared coloring sheets, crayons, bookmarks and informational packets for each of the children. The two men won our hearts as they chatted with us and continued their welcome.

Lester and Rick became Lee State Park for us. Their sincerity and happiness warmed the stone picnic shelters and gave comfort to the shadows of the low hanging trees. Visiting with Lester and Rick remains one of the brightest highlights of our entire Outsider journey.

Reluctantly, we left our new friends so they could close the shop for the night. We explored the trails and the boardwalk. We picnicked at the shelter. I watched the children playing among the grandfatherly trees

laden with Spanish moss. We crossed the bridge, skirted the pond and discovered the two artesian wells that flowed freely and gently with a steady consistent force into the pond below. What delight shone on my children's faces as they splashed themselves and each other with the ice cold water from the wells! The spirit of Lee laughed along with the children and smiled with each successive splash. Lee lives to refresh and to restore. Lee's culture is that of love.

14

ACCIDENTALLY IN LOVE... DREHER ISLAND STATE PARK

I did not mean to love it. Honestly, I didn't even like it. Dreher Island is a nice enough place. I would have grudgingly admitted that much...if you like to fish. I don't. The concept of fishing is nice. It brings back memories of the Andy Griffith Show and watching Opie and his dad meandering to the water with fishing poles loosely thrown over their shoulders in a quaint world drained of color. The concept of fishing resonates with relaxation, quiet sleepy afternoons and communion with nature.

The reality of fishing for me is much different. When I was little, I answered the lake's call and caught a mammoth fresh water snapping turtle. Because I was about eight at the time, the beast appeared to be a living remnant from the Jurassic Period escaped from the La Brea Tar Pits whose purpose it was to capture my line and to warn me of the hubris of trying to lure any lake creature into harm's way ever again. The warning mostly stuck. Once as a newlywed, I accompanied my husband on an impromptu fishing excursion. I refused to touch a worm. I could not agree to impale this creature much less to drown it. No worm need fear me. My husband did bait a line with something fake for me to cast. I caught a pine tree.

I again abandoned angling but would occasionally hold a pole and try to look cool. For me, fishing was smelly and gross. It involved worms and dirt and mud and ....well...fish. It also involved...waiting. Vast expanses of time spent standing still, sitting motionless, letting the quiet seep around and invade you. This was impossible for my busy spirit.

I am not quiet. My personality bids me always move, always stay alert, always be drawn to conversation. I love nature for its life, its incessant movement and noise. The concept of being still and waiting for a fish to fancy a bit of a recently tortured and mangled worm is less than appealing.

Dreher Island was a park I had written off as a "boat dock." It was a pity as this park was so close to our home. With all the truly wonderful parks in the mountains and on the coast, with the many historical and cultural sites, why was I closest to Dreher?

And yet, proximity begs one take notice. It was impossible for me to fly to the mountains and back during the day while my children were at school. I could easily escape to Dreher Island. Proximity begged and logic beckoned and finally I listened. I began to spend my days at Dreher Island. I wandered trails, listened to the birds call and screech at one another and watched as the squirrels bantered and knocked loose branches in their hurry. I saw deer - silent, gentle, alert creatures with deep brown eyes watching me and assessing any potential danger.

Slowly, Dreher Island grew into much more than just a boat dock. It

became a place of quiet repose and gentle respite. I bathed in the incessant movement and constant noise of nature. It was a perfect tonic for one who craved stillness and motion - peace and activity. I could not walk by the shore and not be entertained by the water ballet of dozens of fish who at first alerted and held their position. The schools soon resumed their delightful dance and gurgled fish giggles at the silly notion that they should fear me.

I used to cringe when I told people that Dreher Island was my home park. Proximity begets encounter and encounter begets mingling. Mingling begets friendship and over time, friendship turns to love.

15

PART OF POINSETT

Who knew that such a gem as Poinsett State Park lay in wait for us just an hour and a half away from our home?

We were first drawn to Poinsett when we saw that it was host to a portion of the Palmetto Trail which is South Carolina's response to the Appalachian Trail. The Palmetto Trail connects the upstate of South Carolina with its coast. Our interest was heightened further when we learned that Poinsett was one of South Carolina's original state parks built by the CCC.

Since that first visit, we have come back several times to explore all the park has to offer. We have seen Poinsett experience every season. We have admired the welcoming coquina office, the large picnic shelters and the grand spillway which were all created by the Civilian Conservation Corps. We have trekked around the pond and spied such wonders as giant tadpoles and small silent alligators patrolling their waters. Thoreau was thrilled to see a water snake gracefully propelling itself through the water weeds by the shore.

Poinsett provided a wonderful place for the children to practice their hiking skills. The switchbacks along the steep ascents of the monandock and the answering descents prepared them for the more challenging trails at Paris Mountain and Table Rock. Poinsett is full of surprise. The monandnock itself is a surprise. Right in the middle of the mostly flat midlands, a small but rugged mountain shows herself adorned in pine forest and holly. The terrain actually reminds me of the mountain trails of Tennessee where I first learned to love the woods.

Every time we go to Poinsett, we see others who are enjoying her too. A few families picnic or relax by the water. Many more families are hiking. The lower trails welcome all ages and experience levels. It would take a determined and obstinate mind to steadfastly deny the desire to explore the shaded gentle low trail that circles the water and urges the hiker to spy on the wooded world. We could not resist. We still can't. We follow Poinsett's call and discover new secrets with each visit. We see the abandoned steps leading from the water and quietly watch until we see the glint of the sun on the back of a snake gliding over the rocks. Quick as a blink, she is gone in search of prey. We watch the water through the trees and see a turtle bob its head. We walk through the woods and feel surrounded as the soft evening light filters through the trees. The twilight holds us gently in the now golden air. We are part of the trail; we are part of this place. Poinsett holds us all together and grows us as one adventuresome troupe of outsiders.

16

DISCOVERING PEACHES AT CROFT STATE PARK

Croft had first caught our attention when Wet Foot had a social studies project about South Carolina's involvement in World War 2. Croft had been an army training facility back in the day but any traces of that history had now been relegated to the memories of old men. Croft was now one of the 47 South Carolina State Parks. Croft demanded our presence to obtain her stamp so that we could realize our goal of becoming Ultimate Outsiders.

Croft surprised us as we joined a long line of cars, trucks and trailers each seeking entry into the park. Most parks dwelled in relative solitude. What was happening here? We slowly drove our minivan in line into the corral that accumulated truck, trailer and steed. Croft is home to a prestigious riding and showing venue. The parking lot was full of well-mannered horses and overly excited children. The horses were amiable and turned tolerant and graceful eyes upon the human children who ran and played loudly underfoot.

Promising our own little ones that we would come back to see the magnificent animals, we went out to find our coveted stamp. We spotted the kiosk and the stamp and then saw a sign pointing towards the woods and on further towards a section of the Palmetto Trail. Our curiosity was peaked. We explored the trail while carefully watching out for any evidence of fellow hikers, bikers or (most importantly) horses. We followed the trail to the river which was flowing high and strong from the summer's rains.

The old army trainees would have gladly joined our afternoon hike. I am  sure the comfortable wooden swings offering tranquil respite were a new accommodation since their time at Croft. We sat and took in the view of the river. We laughed that the children had instinctively sat in order of their age and height. They hate doing that sort of thing. Luckily we got a picture before Wet Foot realized her gaffe and raced us up the trail and on towards a

mighty bridge which was also a recent addition to the park. The trail proceeded on but the rains had left it such a muddy mess that it was impossible for our small ones to go further.

We decided to go back and see the horse show.
The trail wound back around to the crowded lot full of horse, man and child, truck and trailer. We guided our gang around horse piles and held hands until we passed the trailers and were closer to the viewing area. The children had picked a favorite mare while still in the parking lot. Wet Foot had spied the orange horse and christened her "Peaches". To this day, the mention of Croft State Park elicits a yell of "Peaches" at our

house. We stayed for a bit of the show and enjoyed watching horse and rider meld into one being that proceeded to run, maneuver and turn, all while showing off amazing athletic prowess and stamina. We learned however that competitions can be more about waiting and resetting equipment than about agility and achievement. We abandoned the show after about an hour which was well before Peaches was called on to display her talent. It was late and Ben's patience was wearing thin. He enjoyed the initial spectacles of the prancing horses but was now much more concerned with the refilling of his insatiable teenage stomach.

We bade Peaches farewell and went off to find food for Ben.

17

THE BIRTH OF A LANGUAGE-
AT KINGS MOUNTAIN
STATE PARK

It is impossible to explore Kings Mountain State Park in one trip. Our first hike at Kings Mountain was a test of our family's ability to conquer larger trails. The early spring day was uncharacteristically chilly as we started the trail that connects three parks together. Kings Mountain State Park leads to Kings Mountain National Memorial and then to Crowder State Park on the North Carolina side. Our plan was to journey from Kings Mountain State Park to her sister National Memorial. Our little ones would not be able to do the 14 mile circle that encompassed all three parks. The chill was only slight and brought just the right mood for the day's hike – equal parts silly and serene.

It was here on this hike that our trail vocabulary was born. We taught the children to help identify encumbrances for each other. We taught them that hiking and exploring was about more than just the individual. The objective was for all of us to get back - no kid left behind. Still, this was a long hike and it was rocky and rooty. The tediousness of calling "rock", "rock", "root" wore thin. There was a moment. I can't remember exactly which moment it was. There was a moment when "rock" gave way to "Steve". Thus was the advent of our trail lingo.

"Steve" was now code for all rocks of note whether they be large masses of granite jutting out of the mountain whose presence demanded our view and admiration or (and perhaps more importantly) the myriad of small stones and the menagerie of pebbles that littered the trail waiting to roll under our feet and bring us into an intimate moment with the forest floor.

Soon after "Steve", "Bobby" and "Billy" were christened. These were the trees. You never quite knew which tree was Bobby and which was Billy. "Salley" the creek came next. Mud became "Murkwood" which must be pronounced in a low, ominous, gravelly voice that had been invented by Little Legs.

That hike gave us a plethora of trail lingo, our own secret code, shared only here and to you. In fact, I give you permission to add these colorful tidbits to your own trail repertoire. "Gilbert" is the word for trail marks. Ben loves to touch each one as he passes by. Moss became "Linda" or "Línda" to differentiate Spanish moss. A "Garfunkel" is a wooden bridge usually ensuring safe passage over creeks, "Salley". "Simon" is a rock crossing over the same type of troubled water. "Jenny", as in Wailin', was the name we chose for the wind. Beautiful things like butterflies, "Angelicas", and birds, "Whitney" were named. Unpleasant features like poo left by critters were also baptized, "Dudley".

The trail lingo grew over our state park travels. It still does. A new language. A new intimacy. A new secret. A new bond. A bridge, Garfunkel, that we cross together

Trail Vocabulary

Compiled by Anchor, Big Ben von Gilbert,
Thoreau, Little Legs, Wetfoot and Roz

Pinkie Dinkie Doo – backpack
Buzzers – bees
Angelica – butterflies
Mordoor – controlled burn area
Salley – creek
Beauties – flowers
Treasure – geocache
Linda – moss
Mildred – moth
Murkwood – mud
Dudley – poop
Sophie – rain
Stu – river
Steve – rocks
Rhonda – roots
Sylvester – snakes
Whitney – songbirds
Linda – Spanish moss
Chester – steps
Simon – stone / rock bridge
Conner – swamp
Gilbert – trailmarkers
Billy & Bobby – trees
Tooth fairy trees – trees with white blooms
Yertle – turtle
Jenni – wind
Garfunkle – wooden bridge

Another trip to Kings Mountain led us to their historic farm. A collection of buildings had been carefully deconstructed at locations throughout South Carolina and reconstructed to form this rendering of a frontier farm to welcome the visitors at Kings Mountain State Park.

We visited on Children's Day. Volunteers manned the sites throughout the farm ready to interpret their significance for young visitors. Little Legs squealed as she saw the games being played in front of the two story wooden house, "Look, Mom! It's the Game of Graces!" She had gotten the game at Rose Hill Plantation and while she had designed her own rules, she was ecstatic to see it being played "for real" and to learn its nuances. The children also played with stilts, the cup and ball toy and burlap sacks. They raced, caught and climbed. They laughed and had a great time…all without electronics!

We went into the small house and the volunteers told the children about what it would have been like for the children who lived there. Little Legs lit up when she saw the rope bed. "That's just like the one we saw at Andrew Jackson State Park!" The interpreter shot an inquisitive look and together Little Legs and I told her about our Ultimate Outsider journey thus far.

I loved watching the children connect the pieces of the story of the state and the parks. Amazing! This knowledge we were giving them was becoming real and usable and interesting to them. The facts were entering their ears, adhering to their souls and becoming a part of the personhoods of my little ones. This journey was weaving itself into my sons and daughters. It was transforming them and making them conscious and conscientious.

We explored a bit more. The children especially enjoyed the animals kept on the farm. Ben stared at the chickens and tried to make sense of their stiff and jerky movements. We wandered past the sorghum pot, the tool shed, the blacksmith's anvil and the cotton gin. We saw the historic garden full of young plants that would have been tended and harvested by children of another time. We watched the cows, donkey and horse grazing in the distance. The animals had no real desire to join in the day's activity.

So much, yet not nearly all.

We went on and explored the National Historic Site peopled that day with reenactors. We read the signage and learned about the great battle fought here by our own ancestors from Tennessee and memorialized by President Hoover much later in a speech he delivered here. The museum at the National Park was exceptional and on caliber with the lovely exhibits we had seen throughout our journey thus far.

We are not done. Kings Mountain teems with journeys yet to be had.

18

PRIDE AT PARIS MOUNTAIN

It's a what? You try explaining or even encouraging the correct pronunciation of a monandnock to modern children. After a few rounds of back and forth explanations gone awry, I gave up.

"It's like a little mountain in between a whole lot of flat...where it really shouldn't be."

I may be hated by geologists the world over but that definition settled the masses for a while. Paris Mountain was where it shouldn't be but for the prehistoric whim of a random glacier. Since those days, Paris Mountain had served as a water reservoir, CCC camp and place of exploration, recreation and abandon. We had been exploring some of the lower lying sand hill parks lately so we were anxious to stretch our legs with a more challenging hike - or rather pull. It had been a while since we had dealt with any elevation. Little Leg's little legs needed help getting used to the idea. If there was any justice to the law of calorie burn, I should get double credit for managing the terrain of Brisby Ridge while actively assisting a fifty pound little girl over the muddy, narrow trail which meandered up, down, around, over roots and rocks, through creeks and beside ledges. Still, I couldn't complain. Anchor was hiking with Ben. Ben hikes with the end goal always in mind. Here is the trail. I must follow it to its end and then I will receive a snack. Silly issues of individual and/or group safety never cause him worry. He would forever go onward and upward and possibly downward if he was left on his own to hike and forgot to pay attention. Anchor hikes with Ben to try to assure that our firstborn is kept safe.

Poor Anchor held Ben back on the steep slopes and watched our son's feet on tricky assents. If my calorie count was doubled by Little Leg's care, then Anchor's was quadrupled as he cared for Ben.

Brisby Ridge was a worthy challenge. There was chatter among the children but it came between steep climbs where extra breath was required. We were mostly quiet saving shouts of "Rhonda," "Garfunkel," "Share the trail," "Watch out for Steve" and "Dudley." We recalled our trail vocabulary and flummoxed fellow hikers as we cheered for "Salley" when we saw the creek flow at the foot of our next climb. We named the rain as it came to join us. We called her "Sophie" and we were glad for her arrival. She graciously refreshed us with her clean cool nature.

Paris Mountain christened us with Sophie's rain. She cemented our commitment to finishing the Ultimate Outsider journey. We had known in theory the enormity of our undertaking. We had vaguely known the challenge of taking four children throughout every nook and lair of South Carolina to hike and to explore. We thought we could do it. The children were willing to try. They had to. They were broke and didn't have a car. What choice did they have but to follow their crazy parents' latest folly?

Still, this hike at Brisby Ridge set us to our task. Paris Mountain steeled us. We did it. We conquered the monadnock's rugged terrain. We did it in the rain and in the mud. We did it - each of us individually: Little Legs, Thoreau, Wet Foot, Big Ben, Anchor and me. We did it together as a family. We were sweaty again by the time we finished. We were sweaty and stinky and dirty and tired. Legs, feet and arms ached. We longed for the comfort of a bathroom.

Yet, we were proud. Thoreau declared Paris Mountain a favorite and

wanted to challenge the other trails. We weren't arguing. We were laughing and planning our next adventure. We still had other stamps to search out and to secure. We had many other parks to navigate but it was here at Paris Mountain that we transformed into Ultimate Outsiders. It was unspoken but our commitment was real and our new identity was cemented. We crossed Brisby Ridge and vowed love and dedication to each other and to our shared journey. After Paris Mountain, the children told friends, "We hike on Saturdays with our family." We had begun this journey to define those elemental pieces of ourselves and now we had found them. Faith, love, nature. I had subjected my children to lectures about the value of each of these for years but here on Brisby Ridge the content of my orations became real. Our children changed that day. They transformed and began to see the wonders around them in the woods and in each other. They understood why this time and these adventures were so important. The journey that had begun as their parents' crazy idea had become one of their own pride.

19

ADVENTURES AT REDCLIFFE – THE DISCOVERY OF TORNADO TRAIL

We must learn from history or be doomed to repeat it. This is one reason why the state historic sites are such an important facet of the South Carolina Park System. What is true for all humanity is no less true for our family. Remembering our experiences regarding historic homes, Anchor and I decided to concentrate on the grounds of Redcliffe Plantation. (Note: We have since braved the tour of the historic home at Redcliffe to great success. The interpreters were wonderful with Ben and there was no fake food!)

The grounds were amazing. We explored the less formidable out buildings and read the interpretive signs delineating the slave dwellings, stables and notable trees. We peeked inside the visitor center which had been newly remodeled and contained mounds of information regarding the Hammond family who once resided here. We walked out among the sprawling magnolias - the tree that most personifies these old southern plantations. Below one great specimen, we even found a secret hidden treasure in the form of a geocache.

Anchor and I watched our children race over Redcliffe's back lawn, over manicured mound of green and on and on from tree to tree. It seemed incomprehensible that this was only a small part of the property itself.

We listened as our children called to each other, laughing and playing. We watched them collapse and writhe in giggles and childhood freedom  on the rich green carpet. We glanced at each other knowing we had chosen wisely by forfeiting busy streets and screens in lieu of this sweet and simple scene. This is what we wanted for our children, for our family, and this is what the parks, Redcliffe today, stood so eagerly to give.

We stood among the magnolias and crepe myrtle trees in the otherwise still yard of the stately house and remembered our very first adventure to Redcliffe some months before.

We had first visited Redcliffe on a day when the site was primping itself for a special event. I had missed this detail on the website or I would have planned around it as the event seemed more formal than anything our little band was used to. It was mid-summer and we had travelled an hour and a half to visit Redcliffe that day in pursuit of her stamp. We were hot, sweaty, decked out in our hiking best and reeked the southern perfume of sunscreen, sweat and mosquito spray.

I had researched Redcliffe's trails and we had determined that we would conquer them. An examination of our map led us in front of the house and down a stately magnolia lane that shaded us from the beating sun with thick green foliage. Except for our own ramshackle appearance, it would have been easy to have become fully transported to a bygone time while standing under the magnolia shade. We walked on and on under these magnificent trees and all but heard horses and carriages from historic days. They seemed just audible from the corners of our ears.

We turned per the map's direction off to the left and paralleled the front fence of the property. We passed the parking area and seemed to leave our present century completely behind and were now surrounded by the magnolias and the fence to the side, the house behind and the woods just ahead. We hiked on. Even this part of the hike proved a long trek as the property is vast. We walked and sweated under the hot sun. Just before we entered the wood, we stopped short. Even Little Legs thought we were seeing aberrations. Sunstroke? Hallucinations? We passed the water bottles between us as we panted in wonderment. No. These images were real. Now, they greeted us with smiles and waves. Here was a line of vintage cars. Model T's circa the early 1900s processed down the dirt road and proceeded past us toward the main house. Families and children laughed at our open mouthed astonishment as they

swirled dust and honked deafening greetings. Our little troop checked each other, the procession passing and then each other once again. If we were insane, we had all fallen into the same delusion. Anchor and Wet Foot furiously snapped pictures to prove our sanity while the rest of us just stood and stared.

The cars passed and on we went following the trail as it ushered us into the woods. We were lulled as the first bit seemed an easy though hot and sandy walk. But little by little, the underbrush crept in towards us. Tall wispy grass overtook the trail. Knee high pine saplings, prickly holly and literally hundreds of tiny brown amphibians the size and color of a penny inhabited the trail. We inspected our fellow travelers and found them to be froglets. There were hundreds and hundreds of miniature jumping frightened froglets anxious to cross the trail and avoid the dangers of our brigade of hiking boots. Now, Anchor and I did question our sanity. We were surrounded by maybe thousands of froglets and there wasn't a body of water in sight. The trail was almost completely unmarked now and covered with undergrowth. My mind catalogued the dangers we could encounter: ticks on the grasses, snakes hunting the feast of froglets, the summer sun beating down, the passage of the afternoon and us out in a place devoid of cell service. We followed the trail further not knowing but that the next corner would put us in sight of the house. Down the sandy hill and in the full sun now, we followed until we saw the overturned picnic table.

There is a point where adult explorer and adventurer meets with responsible parental instinct, where the weighty obligations of the welfare of your prodigy avails the most avid explorer of their senses. It was time to turn back.

We tried. Our task was not easy. We discovered that we had been following not the trail, but a deer path.

Anchor and I felt the animal eyes of the wild inhabitants of the place watching our group and laughing. We could imagine amused deer and even snakes looking at us and regarding us piteously. I saw it in my mind's eye, the snakes telling each other that it wasn't worth the bite. Rather they would all slither back and enjoy watching the stupid humans try to make it out of the woods. Anchor used instinctual tracking skills to lead our caravan. We both made light conversations and hid our worry as we searched for the trail and civilization. None were happier to find the main trail than the parents. The children had been taken in by our rouse and had not doubted our ability. Sweet, naïve babies.

We eventually trekked back within sight of Redcliffe proper. We checked with the ranger and found that the trail had been beset by a tornado a couple of years back. I had an old map and that part of the trail had been decimated by the storm. The ranger was glad that we got out safely and appreciated that we had made the best of our situation. Our little troupe had named our newly discovered trail "Tornado Trail" though it had almost been dubbed "Froglet Forest".

We cleaned up and cleared out fast as the evening event was about to begin in earnest. The Model T's were parked in the front of the plantation house and we were  noticeably ill dressed and mightily odiferous.

Back from memory and now to the present autumn day watching our children on the lawn at Redcliffe, the manor was cooler, seemingly deserted yet welcoming. The place was so full of memories and adventure. It was almost sad when our children rose from the lawn and eventually ran on to the van for the cooler of food. It was sad to leave Redcliffe that day and whisk off to another park. It was sad until we remembered that there were more memories and adventures awaiting us just ahead.

20

THE BEST OF BARNWELL

Barnwell State Park was one of the sixteen South Carolina State Parks built by the Civilian Conservation Corps during the Depression under the order of FDR. That fact alone was exciting. We had seen and learned so much throughout our journey through the South Carolina Park System but the one story that always stood apart was that of the CCC. It was humbling, mystifying even, to travel along trails and eye the work of these young men from long ago. I like to think that these boys would lean up against the wall of the picnic shelter that they had hewn together and smile at my family as we marveled at their craftsmanship. I could almost see them put up a quick hand in a silent wave as we passed by. They would be pleased and proud of their work. Their labors are not only a monument to themselves but are also a tribute to families. They toiled for the benefit of their own families to which they religiously sent an amazing sum of twenty dollars per month which was their payment for early risings, sunburned shoulders, sweat drenched brows and sore backs. They worked for more than that. They worked for the idea of families. They worked to prepare a place of play for the kids they saw in the neighboring community, their own children that they hoped to have and maybe even for their grandchildren and great grandchildren. I don't know if they could imagine that they were also preparing a place of respite for my family, strangers to them in time and place. Still their sweat beget a sweet invitation to my children to picnic, to play, to rest and to watch and see the glory of nature.

We began to explore the park in the late afternoon. The sun was growing weary and the heat of the day had abated. The trail went around the lake and was damp from the summer's rains. The lake waters had risen and had made for excellent fishing opportunities. Unfortunately, the children had left their poles at home.

We walked past the swimming area and the pictures of the 1950 Blackville bathing beauties frozen in silent smiles and waves.

The park was quiet today. It was not deserted but it was quiet. We followed the trail past Barnwell's near spherical cabins and saw families out in front roasting marshmallows and discussing the best technique for making s'mores. They smiled and greeted us with the customary South Carolina, "Hey!" We returned the greeting but hurried on lest Ben invite himself to their bag of marshmallows and stash of chocolate.

On further, we saw an osprey. Beautiful, elegant and fleeting as it beheld our noisy crew. Our disappointment at the bird's flight gave way to wonder as we came upon a sign warning hikers and fishers of the danger of alligators.

"I wanna see an alligator," Wet Foot repeated her ever present cry. "You're making too much noise! Hush! We'll never see one!" Her own loud admonishments to the rest of us scared away any respectable gator for miles.

On we went marveling at the water and the sky decorated by the sunset. Such loveliness was another reward given those who had forged this park out of its primal wilderness. How amazing must it have been to be surrounded by this great scape after a back breaking day of constructing shelters and trails?

We walked on and heard the screams of excited children. Up a hill and down close to the lake's shores, we spotted a grandmother and grandfather and their two young grandchildren. The old ones were laughing as they watched the young ones shout and dance around a giant paint bucket full of water and fish. The fish splashed the children as the former railed against captivity. The children would alternately peer over the bucket's sides and then shriek surprise and delight as they began to hop and dance around their aquatic prey. It was hard to tell which was more excited or where the greatest amount of activity came from.

The children's mother was also watching the generational fun and saw me smile. She noted my own brood of little ones and judged us friendly. She smiled. The setting sun over the lake was all the introduction we needed. "We really love it here," she told us. "We get out here whenever we can." This park had been part of her childhood and now she beamed as she saw her parents entertained by her own children's antics around the fish bucket. "There's nothing better than this."

There is not a better statement of Barnwell's appeal. I imagine the ghosts of the CCC boys would have taken such a compliment with a modest yet prideful blush.

21

AIKEN'S JUNGLE TRAIL – EVIDENCE OF SUCCESS

Kudos to whomever decided to christen the nature trail at Aiken State Park "Jungle Trail". Who hasn't romantically envisioned themselves as an explorer delving into the wilds and bravely trespassing into the jungle to be rewarded by the discovery of a new species of plant or bug?

Which of us mucks our way through the mire of a morning commute not languishing for a thick green jungle to tame?

Bottom line - The Jungle Trail sounded uber cool and we couldn't wait to explore it.

Aiken isn't that far from the center of the state so it didn't take us too long to get there. We wondered what trials and discoveries were waiting on its famous Jungle Trail. We got to the park and made ready to begin our journey. With steady strides we made our way to the lake and were only steps away from the trail head. Suddenly, we heard a mighty splash which was followed by, "Does your mother know you decided to go swimming with all your clothes on?" A look towards the slow southern voice of admonition revealed a boy between ten and twelve years old, fully clothed and thoroughly enjoying the new swimming area that had just been opened at Aiken State Park. The remark had been noted by the

 boy whose joy was just now draining from his face and was being replaced by a mixture of fear and panic. "No sir," he replied. His look revealed his innocence and his youth. The child had truly jumped into the lake leaving all sense behind and had for a moment been overcome with amnesia of his mother's potential discontent and probable wrath. "She will now," came the deep reply drawled out in a southern twang from his father. The dad stood at the bank looking at his sopping wet son. The man's head gently shook back and forth. His hands held his waist and his own face revealed the question he had harbored in his heart, "What am I going to do with this child?"

Like any respectable parent watching an instance of this nature which did NOT involve my own children, I smirked and hustled the kids onto the trail and away from the bank...lest they too should abandon reason and take a swim.

A sign ushered us to the trail head. The trail was aptly named. Trees blotted out the sun as soon as we set foot on the jungle path. It was well marked and we passed heavy shrubs and tall trees. We occasionally spotted enormous pine cones. The cones were as big as Little Leg's face. On we trudged until we heard Anchor call, "Garfunkel." Wet Foot and Thoreau yelled, "Footbridge" while Little Legs and I responded "Garfunkel."

The Ultimate Outsider Challenge had begotten a language of its own for our family. Key words throughout this day's exploration were:

Garfunkel – Footbridge

Salley - Creek

Rhonda - Roots

Steve - Rock

Bobby/Billy - Tree

And

Gilbert - Trail Marker

Another word that would rise to the status of trail jargon that day was "Rosita" meaning mosquito.

Aiken is built on a swamp. The slow moving water that eventually feeds into a river creates an ideal nursery for mosquito babes. My family and I created the perfect buffet for the obnoxious critters. I do not care for DEET but there was no other choice as seven bloodsuckers simultaneously landed on Ben's cheek. Fearing they may well unite and lift my son away, I stopped and immersed us all in a cloud of pesticide. Its effects lasted about four minutes and then the bugs returned. The swamp water had seemingly provided the pests immunity to our feeble chemical attack to drive them away. We hurried on, quickly devouring foot lengths of trail under our boots and speeding closer to the trail's end. The children were amazing sports about it all. They didn't complain much but played guessing games and sang Disney tunes until we stepped off the Jungle Trail and into the light around the swimming area of the lake.

We were at the same spot where we had seen the father shake his head in disbelief at his son who had plunged into the joyous refreshment of the cool lake. I found my own head shaking as I listened to my children emerge from the mosquito laden trail giggling and playful despite their sweaty, reddened and swollen mosquito bitten faces. I was amazed at childhood's ability to grasp the joy at hand and nature's ability to bath them in delight. I remembered the Saturdays that now seemed so distant when the children bickered with sharp words and dull faces in front of the TV screen with game controllers and remotes in hand. I continued to shake my head though a smile swept over my face. I was so very grateful for these playful, joyful, sweaty, smelly engaged children who were basking in the pink sunset beside the still lake at Aiken State Park.

22

REMEMBER RIVERS BRIDGE

Rivers Bridge State Historic Site pays homage to South Carolina's Civil War heritage.

No matter the ideology, humanity must always remember and respect blood willingly sacrificed for principle. The battle site is hallowed. This is where young men fought, killed and died. This is the site of endless feats of bravery, cowardice, horror and enlightenment. This is the place where soldiers proved and lost that which defined them as men.

This was the ground upon which our family trod. We were walking slowly along the trail beside the battlefield. We let our silent gazes linger on the mounds of earth built for that battle as a means of protecting young boys from bullets shot by other young boys. The young ones behind the earthen mounds sped to reload their weapons and return fire on their peers. The battlefield butts up into a dark swamp. It is a perfect setting for an evil day full of death and killing. I cannot make myself imagine the horror this place witnessed. I walked holding the small hand of Little Legs and watching Ben, Wet Foot and Thoreau on ahead with Anchor. The mother in me reaches out through time and offers comfort to the wounded boys shaking with fear and pain. There is a moment when ideology gives way to humanity. There is a moment when humanity gives way to love.

Rivers Bridge is a sad place and yet I am glad that we visited. Some causes are worth giving our lives for but the cost of the sacrifice must always be carefully calculated. I wish that all who ever sat in a stately capital to make the decision to sacrifice the personhoods and breath of their countrymen would visit such a battlefield. Some causes are worth sacrifice but the cost of sacrifice is always immense. The value of life is high and must be fairly weighed against the value of the struggle faced. Rivers Bridge silently screams out the cost of war.

The battlefield explored and our respects given to those who lost their lives in this place, we crossed over into a place of life.

Across the street from the memorial battlefield, Rivers Bridge offered a playground and a picnic shelter. It was cathartic and oh so necessary to rise from the memorial garden of the dead and to listen as the children jumped onto the tire swings by the park office. Some may think the play area is disrespectful to the site as a whole. Not so! The family area -

the swings and the picnic shelter - pay the sweetest tribute of all to the sacrifice given by the young men who died at Rivers Bridge. I can't help

but think that those young men would delight at the celebration of light and love that rang out in my children's laughter. Many of those soldiers were not much more than children themselves. Many drew their last breath while being flooded by memories of home and family and happier times full of love and laughter.

94

23

THE FAMILY OF
LAKE WARREN

Some will swear that Lake Warren State Park's crown is the beautiful gazebo that looks out over the lake itself. Some will say that her splendor lies in the fishing. While both the gazebo and the fishing opportunities are admirable, I adamantly disagree that these are the best features of the park itself.

Lake Warren's mystique is her earthy knowledge of who she is and where her purpose lies. This park could have long ago given itself over as a quiet refuge to serious fishermen. It would have been an easy and valuable role to embrace. Yet, this would not have been a true course for Lake Warren. She was meant for a fuller legacy. She has opened herself up to hikers that explore her nature trails, children yelling and laughing on the playground, and families who grill out and eat together before relaxing with the community of park visitors gathered to watch an outdoor presentation of a family friendly movie.

Our family first visited Lake Warren on Memorial Day. It was close to sunset and we had been out exploring, hiking and collecting other park stamps. We met the park manager at Lake Warren who had come to check on his park even on that day - his day off. He hadn't meant to come in to work. He was out of uniform, a fact that bothered him more than anyone else. He had been drawn into the park by his love for her and for her guests. He was driven to make sure she was well and that things were running as they should. We met him as he was trying yet again to lock his office and go home. Far from offended at our presence, he approached us in welcome. He stamped his page and then (to her delight!) our youngest daughter's hand. The manager beamed with pride as he told us about his park. His face glowed as he recounted how he had extended an out and back trail into a loop trail when he had first been given charge of Lake Warren. He insisted that we go out onto the fishing pier and look at the lake from the gazebo before we left. He shared with us about the animals and plants we might encounter on our planned hike and made sure we knew where the playground was. The park had consumed its servant, but he didn't seem to mind. He understood the place and was proud to be her advocate and her custodian.

We couldn't help being impressed by the man. We asked to take a picture with him. He was shy saying that he was out of uniform. He may have  lacked his proper hat and shiny nametag but he held tight to the most important piece of identity as a park manager. His heart for the park he served and his love for the guests he welcomed clearly shone through in the picture he finally allowed us to take. His pride outshone any name tag or badge.

Reluctantly, we took our leave of this great man to do his bidding and explore his park.

Wet Foot hoped to see one of the park's resident alligators while I hoped that we wouldn't. We enjoyed breathing in the fresh air along the trail and walking under its treetop canopy. We exited by the playground and went on to explore the much renowned pier and gazebo. It was beautiful but it would have been just another structure had it not been for the mix of folks fishing and enjoying it. Fishermen looked kindly on small boys, some as young as three, who were "fishing." The young fishers were actually running and screaming about the pier unable to curtail their joy at "fishing" from the gazebo. Old men smiled at these young boys as they watched them beginning to love the lake. Serious fishers winked at worried mamas who tried to quiet their young ones. Fishing was important to Lake Warren but family and community were the most important things here. Families walked out on the gazebo and were affected by the pervading air of friendship. They began talking with other families, sharing stories, laughing and enjoying the day outside on the lake with new acquaintances as if they had been old friends. The park held us all in an embrace on her gazebo over the lake. The air was warm with all the things that really matter. We all enjoyed the sunset together as a community before we said goodbye. We gathered our things and prepared for the long trip home. We left happier, relaxed, refreshed and thankful that Lake Warren had made us one of her own.

24

AN INSPECTION OF
AN ANOMALY –
THE SANTEE SINKHOLES

We were going to see the Charleston parks but couldn't. A sinkhole, two in fact, had opened up over Interstate 26 closing the thoroughfare. Another sinkhole had just been in the news. It had swallowed a condo building in Florida. The news was peppered with sinkhole stories that

sounded more like science fiction plots of the earth opening up and consuming the toys of man who had stupidly thought to build them upon the planet's crust.

Our children knew what was happening. They knew why. Only weeks before, we had travelled to Santee State Park and examined the sinkhole anomaly.

Santee State Park was a busy

place. Her parking area was full of folks processing in to check into cabins and campsites. The two people at the desk were working to balance the phone lines, a cabin check in, someone reporting an item lost, another turning in an item found and a family asking about a boat tour. It would be a moment before I would be able to ask about the Ultimate Outsider Stamp.

Bored of standing in line and worried that Ben would clear out the park's stash of free snack samples, we explored the adjacent room. We passed the threshold into a small exhibit hall. The children enjoyed seeing the turtle shell that they could pick up and examine. We continued on and learned something about the Native American presence in Santee before we stumbled onto the museum's main offering.

Sinkholes are Santee State Park's claim to fame. We learned about the underground water and limestone and how the water eventually rips out the soft limestone that supports the earth above it. We learned that when the supports are gone the earth falls into itself taking with it whatever has been put there - trees, cars or buildings. Mother Nature shows her sense of fairness by applying the same rules to all. It is difficult to predict when a sinkhole will open and how wide she will hold her mouth. Whatever or whomever happens upon the unlikely and unlucky spot will be drawn in. The children gasped as they thought of that power.

The line had died down. We got our stamp and began to explore the park in earnest. The trails led away from the vast lake and into a low swampy forest. We made our way down the trail between its guardrails of pine and holly. It led us past several deep and mysterious depressions in the earth. A fence had been erected to keep those guests who were a bit too inquisitive from falling into the deep crevasse.

The day itself seemed so gentle. The heat, the trail, the grass and the trees were nonthreatening. The hole in front of me reminded me of a carnivorous plant - beautiful, powerful and hungry. I watched the children explore but made sure to keep a close eye on them. I was quick to admonish them to keep back. The season had been exceedingly rainy. The underground waters were powerful and the earth was hungry.

25

A DIFFERENT KIND OF PARK - HICKORY KNOB

Hickory Knob is a unique park. To quote Little Legs, "It's fancy." It is the only resort park in the state. The children were used to the usual isolated wilderness of many of the other parks we had visited and puzzled over this park's entrance sign, "Hickory Knob State Resort Park." "What does that mean?" the kids asked. "I guess we'll find out," was the only response I could offer.

We drove past a well-manicured golf course that was habitat to those who drive carts and carry sticks. What a different place this was from the forests, lakes, swamps and historical sites we had visited so far. We drove on and saw a pool and a lodge like hotel. We found the park office and stopped there. We were still in search of this park's stamp. We felt as foreign as Dorothy in the Land of Oz. There was a restaurant advertising their evening buffet menu. The gift shop was next to the restaurant and was more akin to a hotel's necessary shop than a park souvenir spot. There was a polished hallway, restrooms and finally an office desk where resort visitors were checking in.

Anchor and the boys headed to the desk to get our stamp. I was drawn in by the gift shop. The girls and I perused the shelves and stands of toys and t shirts. A line of shirts labeled, "Outside the Box" immediately grabbed my attention. They encouraged those who saw them to turn away from their boxed screens and live a little. My only disappointment was that the shirts only came in kid sizes.

Anchor came back from the check in desk. A playful grin decorated his face. "What?" I asked. I knew that grin. "Nothing, "he replied, "We got the stamp."

My eyes directed my husband to continue his story.

"The lady at the front desk was really nice. She gave the boys some sample snacks from the park. She gave me some for you all too. We told her about what we were doing - the Ultimate Outsider - the 47 State Parks. She thought it was wonderful but wanted to know if we had been as warmly welcomed at any of the other state parks we had visited." Anchor smiled. I understood. There was so much that was different about this resort park. It was nice to know that the spirit of competition still found a home even in this alternate park reality of Hickory Knob.

We paid for the children's shirts, gratefully ate our snacks and wondered onto the nearest nature trail. We began exploring Hickory Knob in the way that we knew best. The trail was beautiful. It led through the woods and on to a vast placid lake. We stopped for a moment to admire the view and to experience the calm. We hiked back, curious to visit Hickory Knob's less famous sister park - Baker Creek.

26

A CHANGE OF PLANS AT
BAKER CREEK

We had hiked a small trail at Hickory Knob to ensure that we would have enough time to explore her often overlooked sister park, Baker Creek.

Known primarily to bicyclists, Baker Creek is humble and non-assuming. The park is only open to the public between March and September. Baker Creek is in a sense exclusive and must be given high consideration when planning the Ultimate Outsider adventure and/or the State Park Geocache Challenge. If we were stupid enough to overlook Baker Creek now, we would not be able to visit her again until the next year.

We had every intention of hiking Baker Creek. We really did.

Instead, we pulled up to the kiosk and saw Baker Creek's pride. At the heart of the tiny park is a magnificently inviting picnic pavilion jutting out onto the water. Lured by her charm, we dumbly followed the ramp up to the shelter and beheld the picturesque lake spread out proudly for our viewing. Baker Creek was ready for us. She extended her hand of welcome and invited us to visit for a while. The pavilion and the picnic tables there were ready for us to rest and repast.

Who were we to refuse? And so, we ran back to the van and gathered

what food we had. It wasn't much – just trail snacks since we hadn't planned a picnic. We filled cups of water and cups of granola. We feasted on dry cheerios and raisins. We passed around a communal tin of almonds and portioned out cheese cubes. It was a humble meal, but splendid nonetheless.

We watched fish jump in the lake before us tantalizing the ever vigilant birds overhead. We enjoyed Baker Creek's stillness for a long while.

Baker Creek stopped us and made us realize that the parks are to be befriended and absorbed into our identities- into our own stories- and should not be merely conquered and checked off. We took a breath at Baker Creek. She had chastised us in a manner so rich and loving that we could not be resentful. Instead, we took heed and enjoyed our spontaneous snack picnic of cheerios and raisins beside the quiet lake.

27

VISITING WITH
HAMILTON BRANCH

I am ashamed to admit my low expectations for Hamilton Branch State Park.

We don't boat nor do we have an RV. These don't sound like deal breaker concessions except that the research I had done of Hamilton Branch suggested that this park existed to give her visitors access to the 71,000 acres of Lake Strom Thurmond.

I had become spoiled by the splendor of significance at the historic sites, made too prideful by the long and challenging trails of the larger parks and recreational areas. I had become arrogant from the varied activities and program offerings at the other properties in the South Carolina State Park System. To be honest, I wasn't expecting much.

Yet, Hamilton Branch called quietly and steadfastly as we pursued our goal of Ultimate Outsider. The GPS was baffled. It had not heard of Plum Branch, the small town that is home to Hamilton Branch. It took a good bit of intense negotiating to trick our mechanical guide into directing us to our destination.

We turned in by the familiar brown sign, drove down the main road and on to the kiosk. We saw a flag and a small parking area which provided access to the ranger office and a set of restrooms. The office was quiet as it was already 6:00. We watched camper after camper pass the parking lot and proceed further into the park.

We went to the kiosk wondering if the stamp would even be there. We were surprised. Not only was the stamp there, the park had also put out a welcoming notice to any visitor in pursuit of the Ultimate Outsider title who might be visiting Hamilton Branch.

Each park has its own culture. Hamilton Branch's spirit was wholly shared by this one simple flyer.

Hamilton Branch's soul is one of welcome. She is the Aunt Bee of the South Carolina State Park System. She is quiet, quaint and quality. The park first welcomed us and then went on to let us know of her pleasure at receiving the new guests that the Ultimate Outsider Program brought. The kiosk display made sure that the park's new visitors knew of all her offerings from the practical comfort of restrooms to the reclusive escape of their campsites. She offered her new found visitors quiet places to fish, little known hiking opportunities and often overlooked biking paths.

Enchanted by her hospitality, we could not resist her charm. In a moment, we had gathered backpacks and hiking sticks and journeyed onto the nature trail which led up to the Modoc Connector. The Modoc was beautifully peaceful. The hike was the tonic our car cramped legs needed as we stretched out the soreness of the long van ride.

We didn't have a lot of time to spend with Hamilton Branch on that first visit. We traveled there again in search of a geocache. This time we were ushered into another area of the park and made another discovery about Hamilton Branch. She is a park that is content to be herself. She gratefully welcomes families to come out and breathe. She bids them play on her playground in the same manner that a grandmother bids you take seconds of apple pie. She is relentless in the offering of her amenities.

We watched Hamilton Branch entertain families as they shared picnic lunches and fun around the lake. We found our geocache and then walked around enjoying the relaxation that Hamilton Branch lavished on her guests.

We left after a nice, long visit, after having spent enough time to satisfy polite decorum. Hamilton Branch enjoys her status as a state park, as a place of refreshment and welcome. We would not for all the world insult her with too quick a visit.

28

THE SOFT SIDE OF
LAKE HARTWELL

It would be easy to misunderstand Lake Hartwell. The park is a personification of the fisherman she loves to host. To those unacquainted with the nature of this pastime, fishermen may appear harsh and stoic. The long far off gaze and the quiet still silence feels so heavy that to disturb it with a wave, shouted greeting or smile seems intrusively, rudely and unforgivably sinful. Lake Hartwell can cast the same foreboding shadow.

Lake Hartwell is a park designed primarily for a very specific visitor. Her

shores were meant to be fished upon. Boats were meant to launch here. One walks the shores of Lake Hartwell knowing there are a million secret inlets of hidden fish caches - sweet spots which always yield "The Big One" to those masterful in the angling arts.

If you can quiet yourself and study Lake Hartwell, you will find she is not unapproachable. She, like the fishers who visit her, has a quiet smile. She shows her true disposition along an unexpected nature trail just across from the visitor center. We set our boots upon that trail and were ushered into Hartwell's other self. She surrounded us with forest and guided us up and down hills that alternated in severity and steepness. The quiet of the lake was replaced by the stillness of the wood. The silence was entirely different but eerily similar too.

We hiked her trail. We saw her amused smile as she revealed herself. We gave Lake Hartwell her due and realized the sweet temperament behind the outward gruff persona. We even tried to fish her shores. Quiet, thoughtful Thoreau was the only one lucky enough to catch anything. Lake Hartwell had found favor in the old soul of the young fisherman and had granted success. With that bit of approval, we felt Lake Hartwell's gentle smile. We took our leave and left her to her long gaze across the water.

29

ENCOUNTERS AT
CALHOUN FALLS

"Dad! I caught one!" Little Legs screamed.

Her loud shriek would have scared the fish off her line had it not been securely snagged. The girl was beaming pride. She had only just flung her line into Lake Russell at Calhoun Falls State Park when the unknowing

gilled one took her bait. It was the first fish she had ever caught by herself. She looked upon her catch as she stood as tall as her small frame could muster. Her self-confidence shot through the air. She had become a genuine fisherman.

Anchor became a fisherman's handler,

scurrying from one child to the next and attaching bait, assisting casts, detangling lines and releasing the small finned captives. He laughed to himself about the stupidity of having to get a fishing license to detangle fishing line. I laughed too. He was enjoying this age old joy of fishing with one's children.

Wet Foot got bored with fishing quickly as she had no luck luring fish onto her hook and had rather more luck attracting fire ants to her ankles. Thoreau was finding a niche. Imagine his continuing joy at finding an activity in which one is encouraged to be quiet and still, daydream and imagine, think deep thoughts and enjoy the stillness of not thinking at all. Thoreau's quietness drew the fish to his hook and he also beamed and brightened as he found success at the end of his line.

I find much joy in the parks. I love hiking, exploring and discovering. I hate to fish. I don't like the concept of fishing: standing still, impaling mouths, dragging scaly creatures from their only known world of water and then throwing them back. Thanks, but no.

Ben and I headed to the gift shop. He was patient as I looked for bargains and I rewarded him with ice cream from the freezer in the back of the shop. Wet Foot joined us and we milled around examining the inventory as Anchor, Thoreau and Little Legs continued to fish. While we were browsing, we talked to a family that had camped for a week at the park. The little girls with their mother had never seen someone with autism before. Their mother looked as if she wished she could hide her daughter's prying eyes. This is always a difficult situation for us as Ben's family but not for Ben himself. Ben struggles with social awareness and does not get embarrassed by undue attention. He doesn't understand social cues. Thank God. His lack of perception protects him tremendously.

Still, I would much prefer to answer an honest question than to endure cruelty from those who do not understand special needs. I approached the family. We talked, those children and I, about special needs. Just for a quick moment. Just to quiet fears. Just to introduce them to the very cool person that Ben happens to be.

Then, the little girls spied a slushy ice machine and tantrumed to have the cold treat. Their mother took the children out of the store after Ben noted that they were "sad." We left the gift shop and its assortment of light up fish garland used to decorate RVs and t shirts used to decorate outdoorsmen. We gathered our family from the shores of Lake Russell and left. We never found out why this tranquil water was called Calhoun Falls.

30

A SOUVENIR FROM
SADLERS CREEK

The weather was changing. Clouds were darkening and descending. They began to pelt us with hard angry raindrops. We grabbed children and fishing equipment and threw everything in the van and hurried off from Calhoun Falls. We still had one more park to complete our day.

The clouds had just begun their attack. They were done taunting and were now rapid firing thick sheets of water from above. Defending itself the best way it knew how with headlights shining and wipers waving, our little van crept slowly and steadily on to Sadlers Creek. The journey would have been beautiful if not for the surrounding monsoon. Still, one does not travel this far and come this close to Sadlers Creek only to turn back. We went on braving the back roads that had newly morphed into rivers. We followed our GPS momentarily out of South Carolina into Georgia. A couple of turns later, we were back in South Carolina and on a tiny road that would lead to our destination.

The parking area was almost deserted. Few were as ambitious, read stupid, as we were in pursuit of a state park adventure. The short journey between Calhoun Falls and Sadlers Creek had been such an endeavor that we all wanted to get out and celebrate under the large shelter where the park office was. The rain beat down upon us but we defiantly ran the few steps from the van to the shelter.

The parks offer such marvelous opportunities to adventure and forge shared memories with family and friends. Yet, some families should never take advantage of those opportunities to get together - at least not without undergoing a good bit of therapy and family counseling first. We sprinted to the shelter only to find a large family group already there. I don't know the details, but the family looked stressed. It had been a long day and the weather had turned sour. The group was now confined into what was obviously too small of an area. The shelter is huge but at that moment any confined area would have been inadequate for this group. Disappointment, frustration and anger clouded together and then darkened and descended. Tempers flared. What had begun as a lovely family get together had devolved into loud and profane challenges as to who was intimately involved with whom and the true parentage of the several small children milling around.

Anchor and I exchanged looks that communicated a thousand words in a split second. We got the stamp in the small store while listening to the family drama escalate just outside the door. "It's nice when it's not raining so much," another customer said. He was also taking refuge in

this tiny closet of a store. "There's a lot of deer," he continued. I smiled because I'm southern and that's what we do. I got the stamp because that is what we came for and I bought a t shirt because this escapade was worthy of a souvenir.

31

MEMORIES OF
CHARLES TOWNE LANDING

Charles Towne Landing was the first South Carolina State Park that we ever visited. Years before we began our Ultimate Outsider journey and years before we had children, Anchor and I had heard of and visited the historic park. When Anchor and I had first moved to South Carolina from Tennessee, we were drawn to the history and natural wonder of Charleston. Our difficulty was not a lack of culture as much as a lack of funds. We were broke. We had married just out of college and I was in graduate school. Like many old school newlyweds, we were time rich and money poor. We scraped up just enough pennies to pay for gas to fuel our journey to Charleston, grabbed the hotel coupon we had found in the free paper in the entryway of the local all you can eat cheap buffet and made plans for our weekend trip. We made it down but soon discovered that most things to do in Charleston demanded a substantial remittance that we did not have. We kept looking. Almost ready to concede defeat and near tears, we finally found a bargain in Charles Towne Landing. It was a zoo, historic site, natural repository and museum for one manageable fare. We stopped at Piggly Wiggly, got sandwich supplies and went to our newfound cultural haven in Charleston.

Over time and as our family grew, we were filled with a love for the place. Adventures there became sweet family memories.

If I could take you to Charles Towne Landing, I would show you all of the sites that we have made our own.

There is where the puma eyed Thoreau a bit too closely for any mama's comfort as I carried my baby boy by the exhibit walkway.

There is where we saw the bear lumber over as if to say hello.

There is where we understood just how large bison were as we stood and watched the small herd graze.

There is where we spent an hour entertained by the river otters at play.

There is where we explored the settlement and the garden.

There we saw the replica of the colonial house and there is where we teased the children about the stocks.

There we explored the marsh point and there we ventured inside the hull of a colonial ship.

Over there was where we saw the re-enactors show us how muskets were fired.

There was where we first learned of the Kiawah tribe and realized what a mighty people they were.

Over there is the African American cemetery where we demanded quiet reverence from our rambunctious toddlers. There is where the silence echoed.

There is where we ambled through the historical forest and over there we saw the sad irony of a pack of wolves in captivity.

There is where we stepped past the palisade of sharpened upright wooden beams.

There is where we walked into history and there is where we drove back into the modern world.

Charles Towne Landing overwhelms its guests with things that once were and their modern day implications. The place pulses with relevance and power. Ghosts speak freely of loneliness and fear but also of adventure and courage. So many voices grab at our ears. We strain to bring order. We strive to hear and to understand, to piece together the stories and to learn from them...because we sense the importance of the task.

32

CHRISTMAS WITH THE BRITISH AT COLONIAL DORCHESTER

We turned out of Charles Towne Landing and crossed the bridge. We joined the procession of traffic through Charleston, found another exit, descended the ramp, navigated traffic lights and turns and passed stores and construction sites. I was a wreck. The tightness of the traffic felt like a noose after leaving the relative quiet of Charles Towne Landing. How could another state park exist here in the middle of all of this congestion and confusion? I checked again. The GPS was certain so we followed its direction. A prayer and a left turn across two more busy lanes and then

....there was quiet. We had been swallowed up as we passed beside the wooden South Carolina State Park portal. We had entered a quiet lane sheltered and swaddled by the shadow of ancient trees. We drove a

while longer and found a place where modernity met history.

I am not being poetic, only accurate. A misty fog had descended over a grassy knoll. The parking lot's asphalt met the grass where couples in colonial garb walked. The man in red smiled at our disbelief. He tipped his tri cornered hat. His companion smiled sweetly from her place on his arm as she showed off her own quiet decorum.

Just beyond the couple were more British soldiers. Redcoats warmed themselves by a fire next to three field tents. The tents were smartly staked but spoke of rough soldier life. Beside these was a larger tent such as might have been used by officers to plan military action. There were more Redcoats inside that big tent joined by a variety of townsfolk all dressed in colonial fashion. There was a woman cooking over the fire and over there men were preparing cannons. There were colonial children playing and townsfolk eating, laughing and telling stories of the day. Our jeans and sweatshirts had never felt so out of place. All the while we explored, the fog fell and the sun moved west as the afternoon wore down.

One of the British soldiers walked towards us. Anchor and I exchanged a glance. How lucky we were that we were inside the same apparition. Still, both of us were wondering and slightly wary of just which period of history we had stumbled into. A brief survey of American history explains our rightful concern.

We were relieved at the soldier's warm greeting and found still more reassurance when his first colonial hail morphed into a modern South Carolina, "Hey!" Today was the day of the regular monthly reenactment at Colonial Dorchester State Park. The weather that had just turned so uncharacteristically chilly and threatened rain had driven other visitors away and the players were only too happy to see us arrive.

The South Carolinian born British soldier told us of Colonial Dorchester and its first inhabitants. He explained the importance of the ground we stood upon. The modern day Redcoat showed us the remains of the

Anglican bell tower and the surprisingly whole remnants of the tabby walled garrison which had been used during the French and Indian War.

We were welcomed back to the warm fire and were bid to enter the larger tent that was now filled with rollicking laughter and activity. The colonial villagers were preparing for Christmas. There was a strong smell of ginger. We looked around and saw a woman mixing up homemade

gingerbread that would soon be baked over the fire. As we walked under the shelter of the tent, Anchor and I happily found ourselves under the mistletoe and willingly obliged the on looking villagers and our own children to the show of a Christmas kiss. A young woman beckoned our modern children to join the village children as they decorated apples and oranges with cloves for Christmas. Wet Foot and Little Legs set to making intricate designs while Thoreau became distracted as his eyes lit upon a soldier's cache of weapons that was leaning upon the side of the tent. A Redcoat noted our son's interest and patiently answered all of the many questions his young inquisitive mind could garner. The soldier invited us to watch the celebratory cannon firing that was to commemorate the joy of Christmas. We gratefully accepted his invitation. We were instructed to walk the village grounds and finish our own exploration while the cannons were prepared.

We were again drawn to the eeriness of the misty garrison walls that still stood centuries after being built. They had been constructed of tabby, early cement made from ash and seashells. The tabby walls gleamed white in the fog and stood prideful as we wondered at their strength which had seen them through battles, earthquakes and ages. Turning away from the garrison and past the busy quad where our friends were preparing the Christmas cannons, we stepped quietly through the colonial cemetery of the first inhabitants of this place and back again to the remnants of the bell tower. No church now but only the tower stood keeping watch over Colonial Dorchester and those remaining inhabitants who reside in her cemetery. We saw markings of archeological digs and were glad that study and recognition was being given to the site. We walked past the markers of the colonial homes until we were summoned back to the main tent.

A different soldier came to greet us. He was in charge of the cannons and was beaming pride at the opportunity to display their powerful beauty. The soldier instructed us as to the procedure that was to be followed. He directed us to open our mouths a bit and to cover our children's ears. The cannoneers were assembled and the celebratory show began. Precision in orders, absolute obedience. Like extensions of machinery, the cannon squad moved around the cannon, to it, above it, back again and BOOM! The gun thundered. The ground shook. We felt its power as its sound passed through our teeth. As we marveled, the team fell back to its task. Members moving about the cannon became gears and cogs and BOOM! Another blast! Not quite ready to leave their posts, the cannoneers progressed to a third gun. Back, forward, above, back and with several precision steps in between, BOOM! A final deafening thunder blew against the chill of the fog. Our little family stood amazed and unable to speak after the wonder we had witnessed. We were dumbstruck. This was an enchantment of the festive cannon fire of Christmas which was to commemorate the joy and cheer of the season. How much more movement and noise would warring cannons have wrought? The cannons' power was gripping. A single blast rang in our ears and through our skulls. How much more commotion would a battlefield of cannon fire command?

We left our friends and thanked them for their hospitality. I held Ben's hand as we crossed the field through the fog, away from the colonial era and across the centuries to our blue minivan. I clutched Anchor's arm and contemplated what horrors those early battles would have bred. I breathed a thankful mother's prayer from a faithful wife's heart and gathered my sweet ones safely into our chariot of modernity and on towards home.

33

GIVHANS FERRY – THE BEAUTY OF A RAIN HIKE

Givhans Ferry was wet. Givhans Ferry was really really wet and the ground squished under our boots. The fact that this was one of the rainiest seasons that South Carolina had experienced in years was more than evident here.

Givhans Ferry embraced the water and her own sogginess. She stands beside the Edisto River and welcomes paddlers who journey via water from Givhans Ferry to Colleton State Park. She welcomes families who splash and tube and fish along the river side. It is wonderful to visit a park that revels in its own identity. Givhans Ferry delights in the river and in the rains that feed it.

The ranger office at Givhans Ferry bears testament to its CCC heritage as does its array of cabins that greet travelers as they journey on towards Charleston. We parked in front of the office and donned our mini tarps with which we meant to become as waterproof as possible. We splashed

in each mud puddle as we gathered our stamp. We soon discovered the park's nature trail which led us down the park road, through a ball field and into the woods. As we entered the woods, we abandoned all other humanity save our own little troupe. We were wet, hot and sweaty. Our discomfort was amplified under the supposed relief of our rain jackets that intensified our body heat and increased our production of sweat. Droplets of perspiration replaced the relative respite of raindrops.

Still, we were not blind to the pristine beauty here. There is a quietness about the wood between rains as the leaves shake off their sparkling droplets. The trail alternately crunches brush and squelches mud. We heard the birds beginning new songs after they abandoned the shelter they had sought as fresh drops fell. We were treated as the trail's special guests and were privy to all of this. We witnessed the sounds, the sights, the wonder and the beauty of the wakening of the wood. I let my gaze fall on each of my children and on my husband who was leading this procession. How amazing was this moment? How miraculous was this sight? All together and exploring the first stirrings of the trees as they woke after a rain. Talking, laughing, swatting mosquitos, wiping sweat, discovering, sharing, encouraging, yelling, "Good Eye!" asking "How much further?" falsely promising "Not far now, " complaining, loving and experiencing....together. Gratitude filled me at Givhans Ferry. I smiled as I saw the wood wake from the rain. I smiled as I saw my children wake to the wonders of the wood.

34

COLLETON WHISPERS

Be careful not to miss Colleton State Park. It is unassuming and quiet. It is small and is primarily known to those who look to escape into the woods in an RV or Boy Scout tent. In its quietness, there is acceptance. Colleton welcomes the wild yells of boisterous male children who will one day become men. She smiles as the wild boys run and shout and explore and learn next to the slow black waters of the Edisto River.

Colleton is so very small by acreage, yet she has a tremendous impact. She has made it her mission to remind boys of the value of the wild things and to teach them that outdoor adventures are even more compelling than the virtual reality found in the screens that hold them captive.

As we travelled across the state from Columbia to Charleston, Hunting Island, Santee and all points south, Colleton smiled and whispered her greetings via her interstate sign. We always returned the salutation, alerting each other to her passing presence as we went on our way. Each time we pass her, we smile and laugh as we remember the sweet moments she shared with us. We remember the time Wet Foot discovered the fun of a simple game of throwing pine cones into the knothole of a great tree. We smile as we reminisce about each of our four children staggering off Colleton's tire swings in a dizzy stupor. We sigh as we hear the children remind each other of the wonder of the Luna

Moth they discovered on the low beam that defined the area of the playground.

Colleton is small, but she is intimate. She is neighborly. She is necessary.

 Colleton is content to whisper an unassuming welcome and to offer her hospitality and respite whenever any visitor can grant her the pleasure of their company.

35

HAMPTON PLANTATION – THE SWEETEST FORM OF LOVELY

Mention Hampton Plantation State Historic Site to anyone that has ever visited and their first words will be, "Bring bug spray." Their admonition will be followed by a woeful recounting of when they did not and the whelps they earned as a result of their fateful mistake.

Hampton Plantation is the former home of such prominent South Carolinian families as the Horrys, the Pinckneys and the Rutledges. At one time, the home was site to a large rice production which was both the fortune and the bane of its residents. The wetlands that cradled the rice plants and garnered wealth also allowed for the

enslavement of African workers and served as nurseries for disease ridden mosquitoes that plagued those first residents.

We had sense enough to visit the grounds of Hampton on a cool day. The mosquitoes were quieted by the low mercury of the thermostat which also helped to keep the visitor turnout low.

Today, we were here to geocache. It seemed fitting to be looking for a hidden cache of "treasure" at Hampton Plantation in front of the grand columns and stately magnolias. We followed our coordinates across the bridge and into the wood. I watched the children chasing each other across the great expanse of the lawn yelling, "I'm gonna find it!" I love those images: the children teasing each other and declaring that they had found the trove even when they hadn't; the laughter; my daughter's hair escaping the bondage of her pony tail and whisping out onto her face. Wet Foot was running now determined to find the treasure first. The boys hung together, walking, running, playing their own version of tag. We all caught up to one another and found the hidden cache. We logged the visit and exchanged our token, a miniscule pink rubber ducky, for another similar bauble. We felt the pride of accomplishment upon the fulfillment of our successful hunt. The children celebrated by exploring the woods and climbing up a ladder like limb that seemed to have been put there by nature solely for that purpose. As Anchor stayed with the little ones encouraging, supervising and photographing, I surrendered to the pull of the otherwise quiet grounds. I drifted towards the great trees that accentuate Hampton. They enraptured with their massive breadth. I could hear my family playing on the gentle limb in the wood but I was fixed here in the spell of my own mighty tree. I was held in captivity under its bare canopy. Looking up and around and noting my own still smallness, I realized that I had found the tree that every little girl dreams of. I'm sure that somewhere on that bark or among the limbs lay an entranceway to some fairy land or other.

My fancy gave way as I became aware of my husband and my children all

racing to meet me in this magic portal. It was comical to see them - to see us - ragtag play clothes, hair askance, dirty from our treasure hunt, shivering in the chill and sweating from running through the grounds. I bet those first families never could have dreamed that my family would be having such fun in their yard. How could they? The scene was ludicrous and laughable...and the sweetest form of lovely imaginable.

36

THE WILDS OF EDISTO

There are two entrances to Edisto Beach State Park. The first turn leads to a darkened canopy, down a dirt road and towards a small building that is office/store/camper check in and ice cream/firewood/ supply site. This beach park is an eternity removed from any commercial culture. The quiet campground could just as easily and maybe more appropriately exist in the foothills of northern South Carolina. From the down home culture of the place, you might question your whole sense of direction but for the sand and shell ground you step onto as you exit your vehicle.

We found Edisto quiet. This quiet was not a momentary pause but rather an enduring silence. The place was hushed and preserved. It felt as if we had entered a bubble that had transported us into the earth's past. We explored further back into the park and into prehistory as we abandoned the van and struck out onto the trail. Oak, holly, pine, and cedar mixed with the palmetto fronds to border and define the ribbon of sand and shell trail that lay under our feet. Vegetation combined with a sky

darkened by clouds and the forest full of wild notes that testified to the fact that we had been transported back in time. It was unclear whether we would spot a member of the Native American tribes of bygone days who would question our presence so near to their sacred shell mound or whether we may encounter a prehistoric reptile idly chewing the foliage of the tree tops.

Ultimately, the trail led us to a marshy lookout. We spied a large group of alligators swimming slowly around an inlet and navigating their way towards dinner. The reptiles demanded our silent respect as they swam past us and up the other side of the marsh in pursuit of their meal. Nostrils and eyes just out of the water, their tails slowly swished powerful jaws and bodies toward their repast. They were hypnotic and beautiful. They were also creepy. My maternal instinct fought my intellect. My brain was intrigued at the sighting of the group while my gut screamed for me to make sure my children were far from harm's way in case the creatures thought my little ones made an easier meal than what they were originally pursuing. I gave in to compromise. We watched a bit longer but my children had to endure my constant cajoling to back up nearer to their father and me. Our prodigy rolled their eyes. In response, I shot out a mama look that would have scared the alligators. My children complied.

From our perch, we watched the swimming muscular teeth in silence until I began to be aware of the bright colors of the sunset. We abandoned our observation and dove back through the trees. The trail escorted us back towards present time and into a world of cars and screens and a drive up the interstate and back to our house. I'm not sure if I have yet forgiven that betrayal.

37

BEN BLESSES OUR HOME PARK – OCONEE

Maybe...Do we dare? Could we? Was this possible or just too stupid to try?

I took another look at the Facebook cabin deal and reached for the phone. I called Anchor. My sweet husband loves me enough to be fool hearted right along with me. He laughed and said, "Why not? We might as well try," so I called and made the reservation.

I had just signed us up to go camping in the South Carolina Mountains at Oconee State Park. Our family could not safely go tent camping as Ben's autism makes him prone to wander away in the middle of the night but cabin camping offers walls that just might make a camping trip safe and successful.

Oconee is about three hours from where we live and is nestled in the foothills of the Appalachian Mountains. The park was built by the Civilian Conservation Corps decades ago as a vacation retreat. It was hoped that Oconee would draw tired souls to the hills that could provide respite and happiness to busy families. That was my hope too.

We were and still remain a group of very unlikely campers.

Anchor and I checked to make sure we had packed the children into the back of our over packed minivan. By some miracle, they were all there. Ben was listening to the music playing in his ears and marking the rhythm by gently rocking against his seat; Little Legs and Thoreau were talking amongst themselves in the very back and Wet Foot was doing something on her iPod. Here we go, I thought as I suddenly realized the absurdity of offering ourselves....our family complete with autism, ADHD, anxiety, teen angst and a mixture of ages and stages...to the mercy of the mountains.

The children surprised me by doing so well on our journey up. The park adventures we had had already were good training for this long expedition up the mountain. We made it to Walhalla and then had to pass out the gum that would help to balance the pressure in our popping ears. As we passed curve after curve in our ascent up the mountain, I heard poor Wet Foot in the seat behind me having a conversation with her stomach which was unaccustomed to the procession of upward sharp mountain turns. Back and forth and around the mountain again and again and again....her stomach was used to the relatively straight ways of the suburbs. Thankfully, we made it to the park and then to the cabin before the battle of her anxious tummy was lost.

By the time we arrived, night had come. Through the darkness, we were enveloped by the spirit of the place. We were greeted by a log cabin rich in warmth and welcome. It was framed beautifully by a lake loud with the calls of frogs and crickets and an immense dark night sky bursting with a million tiny twinkles. Constellations reached out to us and waved their greetings. All was beautiful. All was still....except for the frogs that were bursting out in songs of salutation.

We tumbled out of the van and hurried into the cabin. A full kitchen, a fireplace, two bedrooms, a bath, a living room/den with a pull out couch, a large screened porch, board games, log walls, hardwood floors....it was simple but perfect. After the initial bluster of unpacking and settling in, sleep came easily.

The mountain retreat was so beautiful that it was the next morning before the children noticed our deceit. Beauty was given for a price. There was no wireless, no cell coverage, no TV and not even a land line. We were totally disconnected in these woods and would remain so for the remainder of the long weekend. The poor children were shocked into silence. To be fair, they are of a generation alien to a view void of screens. Questions flew out of their young eyes. What will we do? Where can we go to check our texts? Do you even love us anymore? Why are you punishing us?

Anchor and I reassured our offspring of our love for them and then took them just outside in front of the cabin to their own fishing cove. Anchor

gathered poles, worms, hooks and children and went fishing (more appropriately called line untangling) with them. We spent the weekend fishing, hiking, discovering waterfalls, drinking soda from glass bottles at the ranger station/gift shop, making s'mores, cooking out, reading *Peter Pan* by firelight, square dancing with other vacationers, clapping along to a bluegrass band, rowing the little jon boat across the lake, gazing at the stars, discovering that the loudest of the frogs were no bigger than a thumbprint....and the children loved it.

Oconee as a place personifies love and family. It was created by men who hoped families would find restoration there. You can feel the love of those who created the place and those who tend it now as you breathe in the mountain air. Oconee is a place of freedom. It offered us all the emancipation of the mountain in a way that we could embrace. The four strong log walls of the CCC cabin held our family in safety and prevented Ben from wandering away in the middle of the night without our knowledge. The cabin allowed us to access the park's offerings despite the challenges of Ben's autism.

The days passed and it was time to leave. A family of geese had come to visit the cabin every morning and now they were here to see us off. How fitting. The park that had so welcomed us to itself would not let us leave without a proper send off.

The children were sad to leave but we promised we would be back. We had enjoyed so many South Carolina State Parks but Oconee had accepted us in a new way. We were welcomed completely and unreservedly to stay the night and then the weekend. Oconee showed us that we could be campers in our own fashion.

Ben showed his love for Oconee when he bestowed his own blessing on the park. He has so very few words. The South Carolina Park motto, "Come Out and Play" had become a part of his vocabulary a few weeks earlier. He would sometimes say "Hiking" or "Beach". To date though, only one named park had made its mark so deeply on Ben's heart as to forever stamp its name upon his vocabulary. "Oconee," he said with a smile and an emphasis on the last syllable. The first time he said "Oconee," I was so surprised that I could barely sputter, "Did you like Oconee?" Ben grinned a goofy teenage smile and said, "That was fun."

Higher praise could not be given.

38

TOOTH FAIRY TREES AND THE BRICK MAKER'S MARK AT OCONEE STATION

Historic sites have an eerie air when they are abandoned. Luckily, this one was well tended.

We pulled into the parking lot at Oconee Station and were greeted warmly by a vivacious canine whose job it was to check in each guest. Even though it was only morning, the impending heat of the day had driven away any human visitor or caretaker and we found ourselves grateful for the dog's company. The self-appointed attendant was respectfully quiet after his first welcome. There was no noise at the historic site now save our own.

The place was not eerie....it was enchanting. We parked and were torn. What should we do first? Follow the trail and spy the magnificent Oconee Station Falls or explore this land of long ago represented by the silent yet beckoning brick buildings? The trail won out as we knew that the wet summer had supplied torrents of water that would be dashed among the rocks in a grand spectacle of power and beauty. The falls did not disappoint as light fairies played over the water and glittered over the falls. They were rewarding us for making another magical discovery.

We had found that the trail itself was a charmed portal into a pixie realm adorned with every kind of delightful bloom imaginable each nestled into the lush green foliage of the wood. That alone would have been discovery enough but the trail at Oconee Station drew back her veil and showed off her most captivating secret.

Here at Oconee Station, on the trail between the buildings and the waterfalls, amid the blossoms and watched over by the songbirds, was the land of the Tooth Fairy. The sprite had smiled on us and showed us her  forest of Tooth Fairy Trees. We delighted as we discovered this magic. The trail was enchanted as it was decorated by thousands of dainty blossoms the color of snow and the form of perfect little baby teeth.

 "Look," I whispered to Little Legs, "this must be what the Tooth Fairy does with your baby teeth. She decorates the woods on this hidden trail." Little Legs gave me a sideways glance, "Really?" she asked. I shrugged. "How else would you explain this?" I asked. We have never come up with a better explanation so the trees that flung the captivating blooms remain Tooth Fairy Trees and we keep the secret of what the Tooth Fairy does with her treasured

cache of tiny teeth.

Another trip brought us better knowledge of the bygone structures of Oconee Station. The place was still quiet but this time was attended by the park manager who seemed very wise...he must be. He helped protect the enchanted forest of the Tooth Fairy Trees. On the day of that visit, he introduced us to the silent buildings in his care.

We found it odd that a place that had witnessed the bustle of trade and the tension of a boundary fort now stood so quiet. My children instinctively filled the void of silence as they ran between the old buildings laughing and playing, peeking through windows and bemoaning the inaccessibility of the cellar door. If I sat on the porch and closed my eyes, I could picture my sweet young ones in period garb as my husband and I stocked up on provisions. The summer haze mixed images of my present day brood with those from centuries past.

The park manager showed us another secret of the Station. There amidst all the other bricks that were assembled to form the historic building was one special brick that had been marked with the imprint of its creator's thumb. I stared at that brick for a long time. Here was a marker and a testament to the importance of these historic places as keepers of the

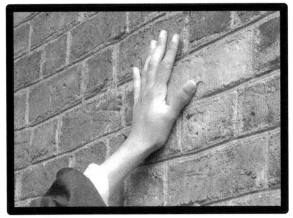

remnants of families and individuals long since gone. The folks that had walked here could not have believed, though the brick maker may have hoped, that anyone today would have given them a second thought. Yet, the mark has been made. The thumbprint is there. The brick maker and those around him were here and in some weird way those lives and personhoods had now intersected with the story of my own family as we visited the place where they had once been. Our humanities had somehow all mixed together through the centuries in the sweat we wiped from our foreheads that day, in my children's gaiety and in the thumbprint of the brick maker.

39
CHEERS TO
TABLE ROCK STATE PARK

Basing our crew at Oconee allowed us to take the time to hike and explore all of the mountain parks in one visit.

We had been told by friends (who knew we had four children but who did not have children themselves) to take on the Table Rock hike and see the magnificent view. I knew my kiddos had conquered a good many trails but my Mama instinct was advising against this one. A smart hiker researches the trails before she takes her four children into the wilderness. I found that avid hikers had called the Table Rock trail challenging especially in wet conditions and had advised skilled adult hikers to slate about seven hours to complete the trek. I went with my gut. We would save that challenging trail for a later date.

There were several trail offerings at Table Rock State Park. We would tackle a slightly less intense trail. But which one? I didn't have internet access in our unconnected getaway at Oconee so my researching was stymied. My new plan was to seek advice from the folks at Table Rock.

It was one o'clock before we made it to Table Rock that day. The lateness of the hour frustrated me. I swear getting the children out the door was always the most daunting task of all of our Ultimate Outsider adventures! We found the gift shop/ranger station. The rangers were out so we inquired about the trails from the ladies who were working the retail side of things. "Do you think we will have enough time to hike up to Millcreek Falls?" I asked. The two grandmotherly ladies looked over our brood of young ones with great concern. I quickly added, "Its ok. They hike a lot." The ladies looked at each other and then at me. They shook their heads in dissent. "I don't think you should take the children for that hike," said one, "but there are a few pools at the base of the trails. The children might enjoy splashing and playing around there."

It wasn't the dissent that was so brisling. It was the speed and tone with which it was given. My children were flat out offended. "We can do it!" they declared as we returned to our faithful minivan. "I want to hike to the top and then come back and tell that lady about it," Little Legs declared.

"We won't go back and brag," the mama in me felt obliged to say, "But we will go get a second opinion."

We found the nature center closer to the trail head. The rangers there thought nothing of our children traipsing up to Millcreek. Smiles of satisfaction spread across my adventurers' faces when they found they had been given the thumbs up. Their enthusiasm made me proud even as Anchor and I apprehensively filled out the hiker registration form that required us to list our next of kin. We left the registration card in the box at the trail head, exchanged glances that confirmed our mutual stupidity, lined the kids up and began the climb.

Though a shorter and less aggressive hike than the one that led up to the highest heights of Table Rock, the trek to Millcreek Falls was not for the faint of heart. Wide trails narrowed and quickly became steep. The children who carried no packs or responsibility struggled less with the challenge than did Anchor and I. Still, we had hiked our group enough to know that pacing was key. We went up at our own pace and made decent time. We didn't pass many other groups. The birds provided the background accompaniment as the children peppered us with questions and interjections. Ben was doing well physically but was tiring of the activity. Thoreau was commenting about every new animal, tree, rock and leaf. Wet Foot was gallantly soldiering on determined to beat the mountain and prove the naysayers wrong while Little Legs was filling whatever silence she found with random questions of great philosophical import. I was impressed at the depth of her questions but found myself unable to answer any of them fully as I carried a backpack full of water bottles while holding her hand up the mountain to assist her over root and rock.

On and on we went. The kids were doing a great job and Anchor and I were keeping up. We were enjoying the journey and marveling at the ability of these little ones of ours. We were dumbfounded at the skills of these hikers that we had helped to grow.

Our thoughts were interrupted when we saw another group approaching us. They were coming back from the top of the mountain. "Share the trail," we directed the children. It was time for a water break anyway. The children accepted our direction and we passed water and snacks among them as they leaned up against the side of the rock that bordered the narrow mountain pass. They were talking and laughing and enjoying this adventure as their cheeks were pink with activity and light sweat glistened on their brows.

We heard the approaching group of young adults and college kids drawing nearer. We could make out what they were saying now. They were griping and complaining about the heat of the day and the length of their journey. Their complaints grew louder and more juvenile as they continued on towards us. Everyone in the group had had a difficult, horrible, awful time - all save one quiet young man who was bringing up the rear of the group. He wore an exasperated expression as he was made to listen to the complaints of his fellows. The group came very close now and we saw them drop their collective jaw as they laid eyes upon our young athletes. "Hi!" cried Little Legs enthusiastically with a joyous grin. A cloud of shame descended upon the once whiny group as they evaluated the children's physical and emotional fitness on the trail. They withered under my troop's childish smiles and surrendered defeat as they panted their way past Ben, Wet Foot, Thoreau and Little Legs- all save the stoic young man who was bringing up the rear of the shamefaced group. He was wearing a satisfied smirk. A laugh almost escaped his lips as he alone returned the children's greeting with a smile and a wave. He let out a lusty, "Cheers!" and he meant it with all his heart.

We made it to the falls and back again. The children reveled in their accomplishment and made plans to return to tackle the more advanced trails. I loved watching them gloat but no, we did not let them go back and brag to the ladies in the gift shop.

40

TRANSFORMATIONS AT KEOWEE-TOXAWAY STATE PARK

Table Rock left us sweaty, stinky and gross. Ice cream was in order. The rangers recommended a local roadside stop and after we had indulged we went off to conquer our second trail and our second park.

We went on to Keowee-Toxaway State Park which had been named for the local Native American vernacular describing this land as one of blueberries (Keowee) and no tomahawks (Toxaway). We should have gone for a peaceful blueberry pie picnic. Unfortunately, we were not that smart. Instead, we sought out another trail to add to our day's collection.

Our first stop was to the ranger station to get our stamp and to make inquiries about the trail. I have since learned not to rely on the opinions of young rangers regarding the ease of trails for a family with small children. This ranger was thrilled to meet us and to see that we were well on our way to becoming Ultimate Outsiders. We were the first he had met in pursuit of the title. He excitedly shared a plethora of information regarding the park and the trail.

While the grown-ups were comparing notes, Thoreau's eyes fell upon a hiking stick. He drew to it like most boys draw towards a football. He began at the top and let his gaze linger over every inch of the tool that separated a childish activity from the call of the wild pursued by men since the dawn of time. This hiking stick - a simple wood thing with a leather hand strap - was the badge of manly sport. Thoreau's eyes fixed on a particular hiking stick. Those eyes lit up when he was told that he could have it as a pre birthday present. The hiking stick was an honor that was to be bestowed upon one who had attained the maturity of his ten years.

Hiking stick in hand, Thoreau strode beside his father leading our party down Keowee's trail. I do actually mean down the trail. The path led worrisomely downhill - steeply downhill and for a long long way. The children were of course enjoying the downward trek as the hike was made easy by gravity's pull. It was a welcome reprieve after our ascent to Millcreek Falls at Table Rock. My eye caught my husband's glance. We exchanged an apprehensive look. We knew the secret - everything that goes down must at some point....go up.

The Keowee trail was gorgeous. Rhododendron flanked the small stream that crossed under the natural stone bridge formation. The water wound around and we saw it trickling in small rapids and then on to a secret set of hidden falls. We followed our trail around and across the stream itself.

A scream! Shouts of panic! Thoreau had dropped his hiking stick into the water. The greedy stream giggled cruelly as it swiped the stick away from the boy.

Just as suddenly, a miracle.

Without thinking, Thoreau's teenage sister, who by society's standards should have jeered at her younger brother's misfortunes, sprang into action. She leaped from the trail and into the stream to retrieve the hiking stick for her brother. Never has a sister so aptly and sweetly earned her trail name of Wet Foot. She loved her brother, cared about him and had saved what was important to him because of that love. If the parks had given us no other reward, this moment would have been enough.

Our legs were tired souvenirs from Table Rock but we forced them to trudge onward and upward to the end of this Keowee loop. The children were surprised by the steep ascent that followed the easy downhill hike. They felt as if the trail had betrayed them. Anchor and I coaxed, encouraged and bribed our young ones until our whole group finally emerged at the end of the loop, out of the wood and into the parking area. We gratefully sought rest and refreshment as we stumbled to the van. Thoreau still held his hiking stick tight and Wet Foot looked at him and smiled.

41

BRAGGING RIGHTS AT DEVILS FORK STATE PARK

I know. I know. I know. It was not smart to add another park and another trail to our day's adventures. I understand the fool heartiness of dragging four children over an excess of eight miles of trail. But the sun had not yet set and the children were game. They wanted the bragging rights that a full day of mountain hiking would be sure to give. I chose to ignore my husband's amused glance as I looked out for the sign directing us to Devils Fork State Park.

Evening brought relief from the full sun. We found even more relief as we descended into the sheltered canopy of the Oconee Bell Trail. Springtime brings mass sightings of the rare bloom which lent its name to the trail. But, this was summer and all around us we saw varying hues of green. We would have to come back to see the splendor of the Oconee Bell. We walked through the wood as quickly as a tired family of six could. We were subdued by our own weariness of miles already conquered.

Most visitors seek Devils Fork for its access to Lake Jocassee. They spend days fishing, sunning and playing on the water. Our trek on the land was

 mostly devoid of other visitors. We finally saw an older couple near the end of the trail. They looked at our children and commented about how well they were handling their hike. I had denied my young ones the satisfaction of going back to the Table Rock gift shop and bragging to the ladies there. I could not deny them this. I let the children recount their full day's accomplishments to the kindly couple. The two fellow travelers listened to the children's tale and were mightily impressed. My children grew three prideful inches as the adults congratulated them. This group of young siblings had achieved. They had gone to the mountain and explored it and made it their own. They were children, yet they were mighty.

42

THE VIEW FROM CAESARS HEAD STATE PARK

Up, up, up, up, up...................

Around and around and around and around and around some more.

Groans from the back seat.

Prayers from Anchor and me that our children's constitutions would hold true and that we would not have to clean this morning's breakfast from the backseat carpet.

Anchor and I exchanged wondering glances that any destination in South Carolina could reach these heights.

On and on and on and on.

We finally made it to the top and found the majestic Caesars Head State Park indeed within South Carolina's borders. Our poor devoted minivan begged for mercy as we pulled into the parking lot. I was tempted to kiss its sweet blue hood in gratitude for ferrying us safely to the top. The heat of the hood and the priorities of the day delayed that kiss. We were off to answer the urgent needs of nature and then to get our park stamp and of course to explore the place itself.

After all of our necessary duties had been completed, we were drawn to the overlook. We joined the procession of tourists towards the steep ledge to behold the vastness of the mountain region of South Carolina.

As we moved closer to the mighty drop off beside the observation shelf, I grabbed my youngest children's hands tight, maybe a bit too much so, though not as tightly as I would have preferred. There were barriers but their reliability is a hard sale to the intuitive nature of my mama bear heart. Little Legs and Thoreau were enamored and strained for a better look. They had seen the sights one at a time up close as they hiked the trails of the individual parks of the South Carolina Mountain Region. Wet Foot joined in and the three of them identified the geographic features they had come to know so well. There was Table Rock. Over there was

Paris Mountain. Was that Lake Jocassee? The children pointed out each landmark with growing excitement while I stood proudly watching and yet still clutching the youngest hands.

I drew them back and we proceeded down a dark metal staircase between two pillars of rock. This was Devil's Kitchen – a cave without a roof. The walls were damp and the temperature dropped as we descended the cold stairwell. The way was narrow but we stepped quietly and carefully through the semi darkness. The family behind us graciously waited and gave our young ones an extra moment of wonder. In all our hiking and trekking adventures, we had not encountered anything as unique as Devil's Kitchen.

We emerged and the summer sun attacked our eyes with its intensity. We stumbled out for a second view of the precipice. We saw how much we had explored during this Ultimate Outsider journey. We appreciated again the magnitude and majesty that was South Carolina. As I looked out across the vista, I remembered each way point we had passed so far in our quest of Ultimate Outsider glory. I looked over at my children and prayed that the memories we had made together would stay with them forever.

43

BEAUTIFULLY WILD –
JONES GAP STATE PARK

Jones Gap seemed a gateway whisking me back to my teenage summers spent amid the Tennessee mountains surrounded by creeks and rhododendron. The park is the fraternal twin of stately Caesar's Head. While Caesar looks down its nose at such surrounding trifles as Paris Mountain, Lake Jocassee and Table Rock, it would scarce admit the existence of its savage sibling.

To be fair, Jones Gap isn't exactly savage…but she certainly is a wild child. She is as free spirited as Caesar's Head is refined. Jones Gap is a lurid sprite who draws company by virtue of her beauty. She is dazzling with her quiet stream bubbling among rocks, a canopy of trees filtering romantic light amid rhododendron. And yet, her beauty is not tame.

Her independence and spirit greet visitors at her parking lot. You can feel her danger as you step from your vehicle. The place is wild and home to wild things.

I felt it. My mama sense sent sharp warnings even as my eyes begged my feet to explore the magnificence of this place.

Ben felt it more than I. His autism makes his instinct sharper than anyone else's. Ben quickly displayed his misgivings. He looked at Anchor and me with disgust as we beckoned the children out from the minivan. He protested as we navigated the path and crossed the creek to the place where the stamp was. His behaviors were so communicative that we almost left Jones Gap without any further exploration.

But the wild pixie is vain. She sent her emissary, a ranger, to serve as a guide. The ranger noticed our family and greeted us with all the pleasantness and exuberance as if we were the very first guests of the day even though I saw that he had been locking up before he noted our arrival. He was so excited to introduce us to his park. He unlocked the door and bade us take a look at the newly constructed education center. The ranger had fallen under the siren spell of Jones Gap and was determined to spread his love to all who ventured near. He spoke to us of the secrets the park held, the vegetation and the creatures. He told us about her past. He gave the children cups full of trout pellets – not made of trout, but rather food for the trout that were held in the park's entrance pools - and spilled all the secrets that made trout the smartest, most athletic and elitist of fish. The ranger walked us to a viewing area where we could see the park's resident copperhead who had taken up permanent residence just far enough away from the office. The snake had never bothered anyone and stayed in her place as a watchful guardian of the park.

Ben calmed a bit as we threw the pellets to the trout in the pool. The children wandered as they watched the prowess of the fish fighting and jumping and clamoring for each pellet. The cups soon emptied but the children's delight had overflowed into joyous laughter. Jones Gap smiled through the ranger's eyes. He invited us back and sweetened the deal by giving us a map of the latest stretch of the Palmetto Trail featuring a long travail inside the wild and beautiful Jones Gap State Park.

The sun was setting and Ben was again becoming agitated. As we drove out from the canopy, I knew we would return. We had been infected by the untamed essence of the place. That knowledge brought a smile of delight along with a shiver of apprehension.

44

HUNTING FOR H. COOPER

We had explored lakes and beaches. We had conquered mountain trails and stone creek crossings. We had encountered snakes, faced storms and battled ants. Yet, this was a new challenge altogether.

"Wear orange," I instructed my husband.

"What?" He looked at me as if I were speaking code.

"Wear orange," I repeated. "The kids need to wear really bright colors too."

"Why?" he cautiously inquired.

"We're going to H. Cooper Black this Saturday," I replied simply.

"And...?" Anchor dug for more information.

"It's a hunting park."

This is almost unheard of. Parks generally combine the beauty of nature with the freedom to enjoy it safely. Basic Park Rules 101: No alcohol. No drugs. No speeding. No guns.

But H. Cooper is a different kind of park. Its full title is H. Cooper Black

Field Trial and Recreation Area….or something like that. I always get caught up in the verbiage and the long name ties an ensnaring loop around my tongue. This is all the more embarrassing since Little Legs has memorized the park's proper name and interjects it whenever she hears one of us stumble around the vast conglomeration of words.

H. Cooper is safe. It is a haven for those whose passion is horses or sporting dogs. Still, H. Cooper made me nervous as I imagined Ben ducking our supervision and ending up in the cross hairs of a deer hunter. To make matters worse, the car's GPS was only vaguely familiar with H. Cooper and gave us what I shall kindly refer to as "general vicinity directions".

None of this negated the fact that H. Cooper was on our list and we needed to collect its stamp. H. Cooper was also very close to Cheraw State Park which possessed another stamp that we needed.

It was wonderful to be able to get out that Saturday. The week had been stormy, humid and dismal. Monsoon like rains had left our own driveway half washed out and had transformed it into a collection of great gullies and hills of gravel and sand.

The drive was pleasant. We passed the signs for Lee State Park and smiled as we remembered the wonderful day we had spent there playing in the artesian wells. As we drew nearer H. Cooper, Thoreau became nervous.

"Mom," he called from the back seat, "I forgot to wear orange."

"That's ok sweetie," I reassured. Honestly, the most difficult part of all of our journeys was getting everyone ready and out the door. The art and science of getting four children out of bed and into the car is a feat that should be included as an Olympic track and field event. We were almost to our destination. I wouldn't have cared if the child had been wearing a swimsuit and a tiara.

But Thoreau sounded exceptionally nervous.

"Mom," he called again, "I'm wearing a target."

I turned around in my seat and for the first time that day, I noted his apparel. Sure enough, my small son was wearing a Captain America t-shirt with a large red, white and blue target shield right over his chest. Anchor glanced back at Thoreau's image in the mirror. We both tried to contain our emotion. We tried really hard….but we couldn't. We finally let go the loud laughter that had been swelling up inside of us.

"You'll be ok, kid," we giggled. Thoreau relaxed and laughed at himself. He must have felt ok about the whole thing because he volunteered to go out and get the stamp when we arrived at H. Cooper.

"All right, here's your turn," I advised my husband.

"Here?!?"

"Yes, why? What's the matter?"

I looked up and saw. The GPS had led us to an unpaved sandy lane leading off into the unknown. Anchor and I grew up in the outer hills and hollers of the Appalachians. We like a good challenge….and sometimes we may not be the smartest. We followed the road/trail as zombie slaves to our GPS unit. We accepted this road less travelled.

It was the longest stretch of road that we had ever encountered. Or at least it seemed so. I don't know the actual distance we travelled on that lane. We measured it more in prayers and gasps than in miles and minutes. This couldn't be right. But if it wasn't, where would the GPS actually lead us? We feared leaving our van's chassis along the sand road as we bumped along to the next hill and gully knowing that AAA would never ever find us here. We wouldn't even be able to call them as all cell service had been lost this far back from civilization.

Man and van melded as Anchor's fingers grasped the wheel and he expertly and cautiously navigated the perilous path.

I did my best to reassure the children and keep them quiet. Anchor and

I were wise enough parents to guard against showing fear though one look through the car windows would have alerted anyone as to our concern.

Finally and suddenly, the sand smoothed. At the moment we had lost hope, signage appeared directing guests to "H. Cooper Memorial Field Trial and Recreational Area." There was the office.

I kissed my husband. My modern knight had bravely and chivalrously born his lady faire (and four prodigy) past the rough dune and gully road in his faithful minivan chariot.

We sent the targeted Thoreau to get the stamp. Of course, I went with him to ward off hunters but I did stay far enough back so as not to detract from the bravery of the moment.

He got the stamp. We got out and stretched our legs a bit. We stayed close to the safety of the minivan. Nobody's going to shoot a minivan, right? We tried to gather our nerve to face the sand pits that lay between this current location and the next park.

We set the GPS and it led us away from the wanton road that we had come in on. We followed the GPS down another trek. This road was still sandy but was well packed and neatly maintained. Here was the correct gate to enter or exit H. Cooper. Spitting child safe curses ("Dagnabit", "Seriously?") to the GPS but grateful that we did not have to face mortal minivan danger twice in one day, we drove off. I handed out peanut butter sandwiches and water from the front seat. We were on our way to Cheraw and the Turkey Loop Trail.

45

TREKKING DOWN TICK TRAIL - OUR ADVENTURES AT CHERAW STATE PARK

Just up from H. Cooper is Cheraw State Park. Cheraw is the definitive South Carolina State Park in that it was the first South Carolina State Park established and the one that made the idea of the South Carolina State Park System concrete.

Cheraw fairly burst with activity in the summer sun as families all around were picnicking, playing and swimming. I could see that this place embodied the "Come Out and Play" slogan that the entire park system had adopted.

We abandoned the van and explored the ribbon of elegant boardwalk that wound its way around the lake and on to the spillway. We loved the lily pads but especially delighted at the many playful turtles which

seemed to swim alongside the boards solely for the amusement of Cheraw's guests. The boardwalk was so serene that I was taken aback at the power of the spillway we encountered. I clutched Little Leg's hand so fiercely that she gave a cry. I held Ben's shoulder and was grateful for the safety rope that Anchor had attached to our son. We stood atop the spillway on a bridge and looked cautiously over the side. It was dizzying. Gallons and gallons of water pouring out and dashing into clouds of foam which decorated the pool below. The juxtaposition of the tranquil den of turtles with this magnificently chaotic cascade was overpowering. We watched for a moment taking in the wonder of the duality.

Ben is never content to be still so moments of reflection are short lived in our family. We abandoned the spillway and headed back to the van. We navigated the interior park roads to the trail head of the Turkey Loop Trail. The trail conveyed its guests through four and a half miles of pine forest, sand and ticks.

We are semi-experienced park hikers. We know to take precautions and to always give the woods due respect. Though the South Carolina sun was driving its sharpest and hottest rays down upon us, we were all dressed to the hiking nines with an ensemble of long pants, over shirts, hats and enough bug spray to fumigate a city block. We donned backpacks and grabbed extra water and hiking sticks. We were ready.

I was so glad that this was not our first experience hiking with the children. The trail itself was flat but it was long. The terrain was sandy and the heat was stifling. I kept telling myself how important experiences like this were for the kids and how accomplished we would all feel after we had completed our trek. We were bonding. I kept repeating these justifications to myself as we all trekked around the loop trail, red faced and sweaty, swatting at the millions of mosquitoes who seemed to relish the flavor of blood mixed with DEET.

In spite of all of this, the trail itself offered its own wonders. There were hundreds of copper colored froglets jumping among the pine saplings. There was a myriad of birds showcasing a gorgeous repertoire of woodland music as we made our way past every kind of wildflower imaginable. This trail would have been one of our favorites if only the temperature had been a bit more temperate and had the mosquitos abated.

Ben's attitude was strained as the trail led on. Not having the language to complain verbally, Ben fell to hitting his own head and then to hitting and biting Anchor. Anchor and Ben alternately hiked before and behind the rest of us. I wondered what we had gotten ourselves into. On we went. We had no choice as we were at the midpoint of the trail. Ben finally began to calm as he began to realize that forward on the trail meant closer toward the van and then on to home.

The trail understood our need for reprieve and at the moment of our deepest despair proudly displayed a simple wooden sign that proclaimed, "Home". The arrow pointed the direction. A little farther and we saw our van. Never have we loved our minivan more.

Ben wanted to climb into our chariot straight away but as we looked at him - at all of us - we saw that a host of unintentional acquisitions lay among our itchy swollen mosquito bites. There, decorating legs and ankles, was a plethora of uninvited guests. We were covered in ticks. The first aid kit came out and we began stripping ourselves of clothes and parasites. I lost count after twenty ticks had been removed from children's pants, ankles, shirts and skin.

We rechristened Turkey Loop Trail as Tick Trail since all save me had gathered a fair collection of the parasites. Onward and home. Showers for everyone....heaven.

46

LITTLE PEE DEE'S GIFT – THE CLOUDBOW

We visited Little Pee Dee State Park on the way to Myrtle Beach State Park and her sister Huntington Beach State Park. I had a good idea of what the beach parks would bring but had no idea what to expect from Little Pee Dee. You could tell where my research had been spent.

Well off the interstate, the road to Little Pee Dee meandered past field after field bursting with white cotton bolls. These fields are the closest thing South Carolina gets to snow. It was odd to see the miles of soft billowy white puffs stretching so far ahead of us and enclosed by a box of grey asphalt and grey sky.

A storm had just passed. I watched the clouds dissipate as we rode on. I witnessed the sun breaking through and caressing the soft pseudo snowfield of cotton with its bright fingering rays. The sun, pleased with the cotton's gentle touch, gained confidence and pushed past several more clouds. She danced among the soft plants and then decided to play a bit with the few clouds which remained up above. The sun skipped from cloud to cloud picking up the remaining moisture and knitting a rainbow wrap with which to cover herself.

A cloudbow appeared. A prism arch of color hung completely overhead decorating the heavenly ceiling with color, light and whimsy. A cloudbow - I had never known such a spectacle. I pointed it out to the children. They looked and assented that is was pretty. The wonderment of the cloudbow's birth was lost on their youth. Oh well, some memories are made for mamas. This was one for me. Little Pee Dee will always be the home of the southern snow and the mysterious cloudbow.

We did travel on to the park itself. Little Pee Dee took us in with welcoming grace. The children played on the playground and we all explored down and around the lake and on to the spillway. We watched the other families. A couple of men were quietly fishing while another family was celebrating a young boy's birthday. Ben hungrily eyed the cake. "Not today, kid," I replied to his questioning glance. I gave him some granola that we had brought with us. It wasn't cake, but it was something. Ben was satisfied. It was food.

Anchor and I led our group into the woods to explore the nature trail. The passage into the forest was flat and easy. There was quick access to the road but we still felt secluded among the pine and holly. A short, quiet explore - legs stretched - stamp gathered and the beauty of the cloudbow etched into my memory. It was time to go.

DOG-GONE GOOD GRANOLA
"Better than chocolate!!!!!"

Ingredients:

Measured:
> 8 cups of oats
> ½ cup of brown sugar
> ¾ cup honey
> ½ - ¾ cup of oil (we use olive)

> 1 ½ cups of flour
> 2 cups of raisins, cranberries or dried fruit

To taste:
> ground cinnamon
> vanilla extract
> chopped nuts (pecans, peanuts, almonds, walnuts)

Instructions:

1. Preheat oven at 325 degrees
2. Warm in a pot all ingredients on medium heat except flour and fruit.
3. Stir until it's well mixed
4. Remove from heat, add flour and stir
5. Spread even on 2 large pans
6. Bake 20 minutes on 325 degrees
7. Remove from oven, let it cool and add dried fruit.

ENJOY!!!!!!!!

47

UNEXPECTED CHARM AT MYRTLE BEACH STATE PARK

Growing up, I was surrounded by sun and sand starved neighbors who made the mad pilgrimage in droves to the shores of South Carolina. Their favorite destination was Myrtle Beach. It is nigh impossible to find a refrigerator in East Tennessee unadorned by a gaudy magnet proclaiming the greatness of Myrtle.

That is why I had sworn the place off. I was arrogantly and annoyingly smug that I had lived in South Carolina for 18 years and had never set foot on the sands of the playground of my home folk. I justified my opinion by stacking up facts regarding crowds and congestion. In reality, I just love doing my own thing and hate giving the slightest hint of conformity.

Alas, it was impossible to become an Ultimate Outsider without checking off the parks of the coastal region. We put it off until our list of South Carolina State Parks lacked only those few check offs. All right. Fine. I was ready to suck up my pride and just go.

I was not a happy camper. My stubbornness at delaying this upper coastal region left us travelling in the height of the crowds in the heat of the summer. I groaned audibly as I looked at all of the cars from Tennessee and other states west and north joining us en route to the

Atlantic. The throngs gobbled us up and together we were processed through artificial lane shifts as South Carolina strove to improve the interstate in hopes of one day better accommodating those who made this journey. I did applaud the thought and the effort but I could not understand the timing of the project which was begun during the peak summer season and added another degree of difficulty to the already tedious expedition to Myrtle Beach.

The journey should have taken a bit over three hours. The traffic, construction and general havoc of vacation season lengthened our excursion from three hours to five. We were all tired and cranky by the time we found the brown sign marking the turn into Myrtle Beach State Park. Our moods softened as we entered the park property. Immediately, we were shaded by the wilderness the park had preserved and then serenaded by bird song. It seemed that in the span of one turn and one curve, we had abandoned the gaudy commercial district and come into an entirely unique place. It was distinct to itself but familiar and keeping with all the parks we had visited thus far. I repented my crummy attitude and let myself be baptized by the gentle air of the coastal wilderness. I was so thankful for the presence of this place, this enclave of peace that dwelt in a community that needed it the most.

I was surprised to learn that Myrtle Beach State Park was one of the original projects of the Civilian Conservation Corps in South Carolina. The young men built the pier, a boardwalk and cabins to welcome those who travelled here. Before we visited the park, I wondered how it would be different from all of the developments surrounding it. I was worried that a park would be lost among all the resorts clamoring for tourists' attentive wallets.

I needn't have worried. I had underestimated the strength of Myrtle Beach State Park. Visitors are embraced by the old oaks and gently led past the dunes to the natural wonder of the beach and the mightiness of the ocean. The education center is situated just beside the campgrounds. Rangers recruit young sightseers and teach them all about the mysteries of the maritime forest and the brilliance of the marine environment.

We stumbled into a class about skates and rays of which we were totally ignorant. My children could hold their own in any class about mountain wonders but information about these underwater ocean lifeforms was altogether new and exciting. I sat in the class with Little Legs and Thoreau while Anchor and Wet Foot accompanied Ben on a walk through the campgrounds. We marveled at how capable the young ranger was who led the class. She was good - really good. She kept the interest and attention of a room full of mixed age boys and girls and their families. She conveyed facts while she passed on her passion. The children wondered as they stroked the artifacts and acted out the behavior of aquatic animals which of course led them to ask a slew of questions. The class ended and the children in the room hungrily begged for the next instruction. They asked when they could come again. They argued with their parents who had the silly notion that they would be allowed to lazily

spend their days sunbathing and swimming. For just a moment, these children were more interested in learning about rays and skates than on lying out in the sand.

I went with Little Legs and Thoreau to explore the nature center which was staffed, accessible, friendly and built to teach and to inspire. The rangers here really cared about education. That was so unexpectedly amazing. I had been jaded by the commercial reputation of the destination of Myrtle Beach. Who knew that the park could redefine a whole community in such a way? Myrtle Beach now brings connotations and memories of education, exploration and restoration.

We were taken into the kinship of the park as we visited the gift shop. Our sweet brood is not a quiet bunch. The children opened the door and their eyeballs alighted upon the ice cream counter. Mouths fell open. Drool puddled and the begging commenced. The softness of my maternal heart could not resist fulfilling their pleas of a cool treat on such a hot day. An older gentleman with a grandfatherly smile and a forearm that Popeye would envy, stacked cones overflowing with varying flavors of ice cream goodness and then bequeathed the treasures on to us. We

 asked him how business was. He laughed, smacked his bulging forearm and confirmed that the ice cream business was a great workout.

In the midst of the mad hullabaloo of the shop, all the employees in the store welcomed us with smiles and well wishes. They told us about their families and asked about ours. They talked to the children and then - in the midst of the crowd and the heat and the mad busyness – those sweet shopkeepers did something completely innovative and endearing.

They listened to the kids. They listened to my children's questions and stories and jokes. As they inclined their ears and opened their spirits, the amazing staff instantly transformed the image of Myrtle Beach from commercial to community....all while scooping ice cream.

48

FULFILLMENT OF A DREAM AT HUNTINGTON BEACH – GATORS!!!!

It was with reluctance that we left Myrtle Beach State Park. The necessity of visiting another park, Huntington Beach, located nearby in Murrells Inlet, finally drew us away.

The children would never admit to being tired but the car got progressively quieter as we made the short drive through Garden City. It didn't take long to see the turn that led us off the highway and onto the grounds of Huntington Beach. We were immediately grateful to again abandon modernity and enter into the canopied shelter of oak and pine. On we drove until we approached a long bridge over a marshy waterway. I heard Wet Foot's gentle sleeping breath from the back seat of the van. I smiled at the sweetness of my daughter and let my eyes wander through the window and into the marsh. I stopped short when my gaze fell upon the reptilian residents of the marsh. ALLIGATORS! Well away from us but along both sides of the bridge, there were lots and lots of alligators. They were sunning, swimming, yawning and posing for the cameras of park visitors standing from the observation points above.

"Sweetie! Honey! Wake up!" We tried our best to rouse the sleeping Wet Foot but our attempts were futile. Exhaustion and a sugar crash had made her near comatose.

Wet Foot had spent the greater part of our Ultimate Outsider journey whining, complaining, begging and praying....dying to see alligators. Most alligators had been smart enough to steer clear of our noisy brood (save at Edisto)...but here at Huntington Beach, we were fairly surrounded by the aquatic beasts and Wet Foot was missing it!

Only after we pulled up to the gift shop/park office and the gentle rocking of the van quieted, did the child stir. The poor thing was almost in tears when we told her what she had missed. Of course, it didn't help that her siblings relentlessly tortured her with minute details of the gator sighting. I couldn't bear it for Wet Foot. In sympathy, I delivered a stern stare accompanied by a no nonsense direction for the tormentors to cease aggravating their sister.

Everyone was soon distracted by the beach itself. It is amazing that Huntington is so geographically close to Myrtle Beach and yet so culturally different. Huntington Beach quickly won our hearts with its unassuming wild spirit. The commercial development was further removed here and harder to spot. Both beaches played host to lots of visitors that day and both parks attracted all age groups. Still, something was acutely different. Myrtle Beach vibrated with vacation excitement. It burst with noise, movement and freedom. Huntington felt more subdued. Perhaps the beach absorbed some of the quietness of Atalaya, the abandoned castle of Anna Hyatt Huntington who had once used the entire property of the park as a retreat to feed the creativity that she then poured into the sculptures she created. Perhaps the difference was the relative distance from the main strip. Whatever the reason, Huntington's relaxing gentle invitation was a perfect complement to the hustle of the vitality of Myrtle Beach.

We spent a long time on the beach and even my mountain heart was won over by Huntington's rhythmic waves. Ben and I walked along the beach as Anchor played in the ocean with our other children. I heard their laughter behind me. I was content to quietly walk alongside Ben. Ben is not a creature of stillness - neither am I. We move even when we are peaceful. I stayed with Ben so he would walk along the shore and not challenge the tide and walk out to drown. We walked on and on in the soft squishy sand as the water came up to our ankles. We saw boats and fish and birds. We gathered shells and greeted fellow explorers. "Hello there," was the greeting Ben offered most often. Eventually, we turned back to check on the others. They were having a blast constructing castles with the moist sand left over from the tide. My tranquil smile met excited screams of laughter as Ben and I were bombarded with exultations recounting ocean adventures encountered during our short absence.

The afternoon stretched out. Sunset came and we were off - back to the interstate and a three hour drive home. There was too much to see here. We would have to come back to explore Atalaya and the incredible nature center here too.

But- for Wet Foot - we made one pause before we started back. We stopped to spy the great reptiles who hid in the marsh under the bridge in front of the spectacular backdrop of the sunset. Her dreams of admiring alligators were fulfilled in that moment just beside the marshes of Huntington.

49

THE FIRST FAMILY OF ULTIMATE OUTSIDERS! OUR CHRISTENING AT HUNTING ISLAND!

We drove forever. Then we drove some more. We drove and drove and drove and drove. Beaufort is one of the most remote points of our state if you don't live there to start with...and St. Helena is even beyond that.

I had heard of Hunting Island's raw loveliness and of its eerie bone yard. That beauty had never before bribed me into making this tremendous campaign to the outer edge of the state with four children. I can appreciate beauty from afar. I can respect culture without having to experience it firsthand.

Still, I am a sucker for a challenge. Hunting Island was our last park left to visit before we would become South Carolina's First Ever Ultimate Outsiders! The nearness of the title and all associated glory (a cool t shirt and substantial bragging rights) dragged me from my cozy bed and onto the interstate all the way down to the barrier islands.

Hunting Island sounds as if it is a secluded place and it is aptly named. We spotted the brown park sign about a half hour after abandoning all traces of human habitat or accessible public bathrooms. The latter was of particular import to Wet Foot who had finished her water bottle some time before and was beset by the urge to relieve herself just after we passed the threshold from humanity into nothingness. When we were fairly convinced that the next turn off from the highway would throw us into the Atlantic, we arrived at Hunting Island State Park. We toured the park first by car as we lost our way through the internal labyrinth of park roads. A couple of minutes later, which seemed like two eternities to poor Wet Foot, we successfully solved the maze and made our way to the ranger station which provided a place to park our faithful chariot.

Wet Foot quickly ran on ahead to find the welcome relief of clean bathrooms. Soon, everyone was inside the building and had attended to all our personal needs. Not quite knowing how to proceed, we gathered together at the front desk. It was such a surreal moment. We all stood there, Anchor, me, Ben, Wet Foot, Thoreau and Little Legs, waiting expectantly as the ranger came out of her office and approached us. The ranger, quiet, capable and shy, took a step back as she observed this family who lost their minds as soon as she applied her stamp to our paper. This was not a time for decorum. We partied right there and shattered the silence of the near empty and ever so official ranger station. Hugs, high fives, wild yells mixed with joyous laughter as we relished in our accomplishment. Not only had we conquered the challenge of exploring each of South Carolina's 47 State Parks, but we were the first ones to fulfill the requirements of this program. We were South Carolina's First Family of Ultimate Outsiders.....and it was AWESOME! The ranger really didn't know what to think. She stood there watching our instant party and wondering whether or not she should have us removed from the station if not from the park itself. We didn't care. Our sanity has been questioned before over less expressive outbursts. This moment was worth celebrating! After all our travels and all of our efforts, we deserved any pomp and circumstance we decided to bestow upon ourselves.

After several minutes, we gained just enough composure to ask how to get to the beach. The ranger, still watching this odd family with wide wondering eyes, gladly told us where it was. I suspect she drew a relieved breath as we left.

We made haste and were soon at the beach parking lot. We walked past the park's one visitor cabin just beside the focal point of the property, the only historic lighthouse accessible to the public in South Carolina. We eyed both cabin and lighthouse from a distance but left both unexplored. Today was our celebration day and a climb up the lighthouse steps in the South Carolina summer heat seemed entirely too much work. Besides, Ben was already pulling hard on my arm and pointing past the monument directing me on towards his goal, "Beach." We walked on and then stood on the wet sand of the low tide.

Hunting Island's charm is heightened by her remoteness. She stands by herself unmolested by evidence of the unsightly greedy air of commercial development. The Atlantic kisses the coast

of Hunting Island and decorates her shore with sea foam, shells and shark teeth. Needing to extend the grace of the island's relative solitude, we walked on past the other tourists on the beach. The parks had gifted us with a fondness for solitude. We basked in the isolation of the island as we explored a forest of wild wooden juttings of washed up wood that had been bleached by the sun and the surf and were now referred to as the

"bone yard." We climbed and played amid the ghostly wood in the haunted forest on the sand. Our laughter echoed against the ocean as we explored the barkless wonders on her shore.

As we made our way through these island furnishings, our eyes were drawn to a collection of tiny black daggers in the sand. I had never before seen a single solitary shark's tooth except in tourist shops but here on the beach were at least a dozen that had been washed ashore for our benefit. The children delighted in the discovery! Elation! Laughter! Accomplishment! Youthful joyous screams! I joined in the search but couldn't repress my own giggles as I imagined an ocean full of toothless sharks gumming swordfish.

Hours passed as we played to the background music of the rhythmic waves, calling gulls and our own wild sounds as we reveled in the splendor of the beach and the gladness of each other's company. What a fitting way to end our Ultimate Outsider journey. We had been transformed as a family and the laughing tide baptized us as a new entity all together. The sand and saltwater christened us Ultimate Outsiders who embraced life outside the current cultural norms. We had left status quo behind when we had realized how paralyzing and debilitating it was. We had purposely chosen the wilds over the malls, the company of one another over that of avatars and the wonder of reality over a fictitious world. We had become Ultimate Outsiders and crossed into a world of discovery, exploration, experience and intimacy.

I looked around and beheld this changed family. We had changed in ways we never could have fathomed. I looked around and watched with a grateful and overflowing heart. I was more than satisfied. I watched the children playing with each other against the backdrop of a glorious sunset. I was satisfied. This whole experience had been worth it. I thought of all of the reasons we had begun this journey. A smile stole over me and could not be driven from my face. I relished this one moment. Here, now, I had my children back.

50

JOURNEY'S END...
NEW LIFE BEGUN

Ummmmmmmm......no. There was no way that I was going to hand over our precious ragged notebook of stamps collected from 47 parks scattered all over the state of South Carolina to anyone but the central park office.

It made no sense. Our family had ventured out to every nook and cranny of the state. We had driven down paved, dirt, gravel, sand and pseudo roads through towns with barely a stop light to their credit. We had explored swamps, lakes, sand hills, mountains and shores. We had discovered Carolina Bays, monadnocks and sinkholes. We had dedicated ourselves to this Ultimate Outsider Challenge. Bless their hearts for their intent, but there was never a question in our minds. We were personally taking our collection of qualifying stamps to the State House.

It was the right way to cap this leg of our journey. The South Carolina

Park System operates the tourism piece of the State House. The South Carolina State House is in theory and in practice the 48th South Carolina State Park. We could not deny ourselves.

Arrangements were made. We donned our best park t-shirts and carefully gathered what we would need for our journey.

This was our easiest exploration. We had travelled in excess of three hours to get to the mountain parks near Oconee and about the same when we had gone to Beaufort and Myrtle Beach. Columbia was a half hour drive from our home.

I had traded my well-travelled pink backpack for two or three well stocked mom bags before we set out. I prayed for sheer convenience sake that they would not have to be emptied out at the capital's security checkpoint. Those prayers were answered. Apparently a family with four kids in state park shirts doesn't fit a terrorism standard profile and/or security cares less for administrative employees than it does for legislators. We checked in but were not made to surrender our bags for inspection. We herded the children onto the elevator (a feat akin to managing a three ring circus and just as entertaining to watch) and into the outer office of the Park System's suite.

Admittedly, we are......um.......a unique family. Thoreau and Little Legs had worn their Junior Park Ranger hats. Wet Foot was holding Ben's hand and Ben was being kept calm by listening to loud Veggie Tales music via MP3 and earbud. He was jumping along to the beat and pointing in the direction of the snacks put out on the front desk. Anchor and I were doing our best to gather and move our group of excited and distracted children into the large room at the end of the hall while negotiating all our bags and bundles and keeping some sane amount of decorum. The kids were behaving beautifully but still I monitored them closely as my overall expectations were higher than usual in this strange place.

A slew of State Park folk came in to meet us. The director of the parks

introduced himself as Ranger Phil. He was a tall man who had taken the responsibility of the parks for the sake of protecting and preserving these important places and stories for the citizens of the state and not for any great love of administrative duty. He is fully capable and struck me as a dynamic and intelligent leader. He is the John Wayne of the park system. He is bound by his duty and responsibility and love for the parks but his eyes betray his overall distaste for florescent lights and enclosed spaces.

The office was the opposite of any of the beautiful places we had explored. This suite - these walls - were devoid of everything. There was no color save an almost futile attempt of decorating with various photographs from the actual parks. The pictures were a start but served to taunt rather than to decorate. The walls were white, the carpet beige, the air still and quiet. I understood that it was a state office but the place was so very grown up. We had played guest to rustling leaves, crashing waves, gentle breezes and laughing streams. We had listened to a mountain orchestration of bullfrogs, crickets and spring peepers. We had not entered a park that had not bathed us in a sensory ecstasy of color, scent and sound. But this place....was quiet and bare and sad.

I knew the office complex was the proverbial back closet of the park system - where the necessities are put so the system as a whole could work well and be maintained and loved. I just hadn't thought it would be this bad. Still, we were prepared. I smiled at my husband. He kindly did not roll his eyes at me. He just sat back to get a better view of his wife at work.

Everyone has talents. I am excellent at encouragement and excel in the art of reminding people of how great an impact they have on the world around them. What a joy to do that here! The people at the state office worked so hard throughout the year to ensure the preservation of the parks so that guests may come and discover the treasures of story and place. We had enjoyed our journey so much. It was fitting for us to come and encourage these dear people by bringing some of our experiences into the gray and beige walled capital office and to remind those trapped here of the fruits of their labors.

And so....I unloaded my mama bags. Out came the toys we had purchased from the historic sites. Out came the books that Thoreau and Little Legs had created about the different plants and animals they had discovered on their journey. Out came the quilt we had made to memorialize our status as Ultimate Outsiders. Out came the pictures and the tales and the laughter as we all began to share memories.

We overwhelmed them with the exuberance we brought back from the native places we had visited. In moments, the entire staff was reminded of their purpose - to bring people together with the wilderness in the park system, to see the fulfilment that these protected places bestow on the families they serve. They lapped up the children's stories of hiking at Table Rock, camping at Oconee, splashing in the artesian wells at Lee and the waves at Huntington Beach. The office workers leaned forward so as not to miss one word of the recounting of finding shark teeth at Hunting Island, sinkholes at Santee and a caterpillar tree at Woods Bay. Their jaws fairly dropped to hear Thoreau and Little Legs accurately describe the stories they had learned of the Gist family from Rose Hill and the Hammond family of Redcliffe as well as the battles of Musgrove Mill, Kings Mountain and Rivers Bridge.

The sensory deprived staff played with the children and challenged each other as to who could best catch the ball in the cup or command the gee-haw-whimmy-diddle. The children patiently explained the tricks of the wooden buzz saw spinner and reminded the staff of how to play the old card games of war and crazy 8's. An hour passed. Two. We were all having so much fun. We could have spent the day with our new friends except that they were called off to the work required of them to nurture and care for those places that so nurtured families like ours.

I like to think that we affected our new friends - that we showed them

the necessity of their labors. I like to think that those who tended the parks were reminded of the impact that those places, stories and people were having on the families they served. I like to think that we affected them by relating stories of how we had been affected by the parks. I like to think that we gave them reason to work even more diligently now that we had reassured them of their crucial role as advocates of their 47 trusts. I hoped they remembered my children's faces as they tended their charges. I wanted the staff to remember our stories and our laughter. I wanted to give them a touch point - a memory to give momentum to their passion of mission even on the difficult days and through the most tedious tasks.

Our family - these children.

The parks had given us so much.

This day and these memories - that was our gift to them.

Made in the USA
Columbia, SC
23 January 2018